MW01617828

A LEAD HEROES & BANTAMEDIA COLLABORATION

HOW TO QUALIFY, PRESENT & SELL FINAL EXPENSE AND MEDICARE SUPPLEMENTS TO SENIORS

GLEN SHELTON & JUSTIN BILYJ

EDITED BY BROOKE N. BATES

Formatted by Chad Robertson in 2016.

Thank you for purchasing this book.

TABLE OF CONTENTS

INTRODUCTION: WHY THIS GUIDE WAS CREATED

To Help Agents

We created this resource specifically for insurance agents who sell or want to sell Medicare Supplements and Final Expense life insurance using telemarketed and direct mail leads.

Insurance is a tough industry because it's a commission-based sales job in a field where the products and solutions can be complicated for consumers to understand. Sure, some agencies pay salaries, but the majority of agents work primarily for commission. Before you can earn any commission, though, you have to find interested prospects to talk to every day about the solutions you provide, educate them on their options until they make a decision, and successfully juggle multiple prospects at various points in the sales cycle to earn a living as an insurance agent.

Hopefully, this guide will give you a foundation to stand on when approaching senior clients, helping you build a book of business by effectively solving their insurance needs.

To Better Serve Seniors

Although we made this resource for you, the agent, it's really not about you, is it? It's about your clients and your ability to help them solve their problems. The underlying reason why we're writing this resource is that there's a tsunami of baby boomers and other seniors who are retiring soon, and they'll need help with two critical priorities:

1. Understanding their Medicare plan options.

2. Preparing for their final expenses and last wishes.

Unfortunately, these seniors don't have a huge pool of insurance agents to help them with these problems because there has never been a larger deficit of agents entering the insurance workforce.

According to a recent Forbes article,[1] Millennials think insurance is boring, and the industry as a whole is not meaningful or cool. Meanwhile, the average U.S. insurance agent is 59; in fact, one-fourth of the workforce will retire by 2018, according to a report from management consulting firm, McKinsey & Co. as reported by Caitlin Bronson on the website Insurance Business America.[2] These two variables will have disastrous results for seniors trying to find affordable, reliable options for their life and medical insurance.

We created this book, not just to help agents make money by selling insurance, but more importantly, to help agents better serve the needs of seniors during this critical time. We want to help agents sell more effectively, build a thriving book of business, and overcome the five main challenges that stand in the way of being a successful insurance agent selling Final Expense or Medicare Supplements:

1. Selling insurance is usually a commission-based career. There are some captive job positions available, but for the majority of employment opportunities, agents are required to sell and earn a living by depending on commissions. Your financial success is in your hands.

2. Interacting with older people can be challenging. They have repeatedly been advised to distrust salespeople because of the potential for financial fraud.

3. Being an independent agent is a solitary type of job; the only interaction with colleagues happens in online forums and, sometimes, weekly agency meetings.

4. Finding seniors to talk to about their Final Expense or Medicare Supplement concerns requires getting in front

---

[1] http://www.forbes.com/sites/larissafaw/2015/11/30/millennials-just-dont-want-to-be-insurance-agents/

[2] http://www.ibamag.com/news/marine/one-in-four-insurance-agents-will-be-gone-by-2018-17943.aspx

of a lot of people on a monthly basis. Reaching a lot of people can require a lot of effort. This is why it's important for insurance agents to have seed money to pay for marketing, leads, and living expenses until commissions start rolling in. By optimizing your approach to potential clients, you can maximize time and profit by making fewer mistakes at first.

5. The final hurdle to becoming a successful agent is training. The agent training provided by most insurance companies typically only covers specific insurance products without drilling into prospecting and sales tactics. To access advanced sales training, agents have to either produce enough business to get invited to elite insurance sales clubs or shell out thousands to pay for non-industry-specific sales training. It is our mission with this book to provide the initial amount of insurance sales training to get you off the ground and gaining clients.

What This Guide Covers

This guide covers:

- The two types of insurance sold to seniors, which are Final Expense life insurance and Medicare Supplement insurance plans
- The pros and cons of selling each of these types of insurance
- The various types of leads available to insurance agents
- How to approach these leads
- What to say to prospects to gain the trust you need to help them with their insurance decisions

- How to nurture senior prospects through the insurance sales cycle to gain clients
- What to do once you get a client to avoid losing them (or your commission)
- How to grow your client base by cross-selling products and generating referrals
- How successful insurance agents organize their days and spend their time
- How to keep your sales process on track and motivate yourself to perform
- How to create an online brand that will build trust and referrals

... and much more, but we don't want to spoil all of the surprises before the first chapter!

HOW THIS GUIDE IS ORGANIZED

The guide will follow the path of the insurance sales cycle to cover the entire process in detail: from behind-the-scenes preparations, to initially ordering and contacting leads, to qualifying and presenting, and also providing great customer service along the way (and, most importantly, after the sale).

We organized this process into four main sections:

PART I. Building a Foundation for Insurance Sales Success

PART II. The Insurance Sales Process: How Leads Become Clients

PART III. After the Sale: Keeping and Growing Your Business

PART IV. Online Branding

Throughout this guide, you will see quotes from the collaborators who helped us put this resource together. These collaborators are successful Final Expense and Medicare Supplement insurance agents who utilize telemarketed leads to build a book of business in their respective fields. We owe them special thanks for sharing tips, lessons, strategies, and even script examples to illustrate what their sales processes look like in action.

You can see a full list of our collaborators at the end of this book, but on your way there, you'll learn a lot about selling insurance from them and from the other info we've compiled here.

PART I. BUILDING A FOUNDATION FOR INSURANCE SALES SUCCESS

CHAPTER 1: FINAL EXPENSE OR MEDICARE SUPPLEMENTS?

Some of the agents reading this guide are already selling one type of insurance over the other, while others of you don't yet know which one you should sell. There are four significant differences agents should consider before deciding to sell one insurance over the other:

- The size and duration of commissions,
- The type of environment you will be selling in,
- How long it takes to understand that vertical of insurance, and
- The amount of customer service needed to keep clients on the books.

1. Commissions

Commissions are a large reason why insurance agents decide to sell Final Expense over Medicare Supplements and vice versa. Commissions for life insurance differ from commissions for Medicare Supplements in several ways.

It's no secret to insurance agents that life insurance pays more commission upfront. Commission rates for Final Expense life insurance vary from 100-120% of the first year's premium, depending on the agent's experience or production and the size of the agent's agency, if any. Medicare Supplements pay a fraction of that – only 18-25% of the first year's premium, also depending on an agent's production history and, possibly, agency size. Even though the commission percentages are largely different from each other by 80-100%, the average annual premium is also very different between the two. Final Expense has an average annual premium of $540 a year and Medicare Supplements have an average annual premium of $1,800 if the senior is on a more competitive plan, otherwise the average premium is around $2,100 according to a Kaiser Family Foundation study.[3] This means the average commission percentage for a Final Expense policy is 5-6x that of the average commission percentage of a Medicare Supplement, but Medicare Supplements have 3-4x the amount of average annual premium.

Here's an example first year's commission for both a Final Expense Plan and a Medicare Supplement:

The average premium for a Final Expense sale is $45 a month, totaling $540 for the year. Multiply that by the commission percentage, which for our example is 110%, and you've earned $594 upfront. Now let's look at the average premium for a Medicare Supplement plan, which is $175 per month, totaling $1,800 a year. However, since the agent is more likely saving the senior money, he will often be presenting the same plans for a more competitive price (under the average), which we're assuming is, on average, $150 a month or $1,800 a year; it may be higher or lower depending on the area, type of plan (N vs F), or the age of the prospect. Agents working with younger turning 65 seniors will see even a smaller premium than the average. Multiply that premium by the commission percentage of 20% for our example, and this comes out to $360 in commission.

However, most insurance companies pay agents a nine-month advance for selling these policies, so agents get 75% of their first year's commission upfront. A $600 Final Expense commission pays $450 in advance. For Med Supps, the advance on a $360 commission is $270. The rest of the commission is paid in the last three months, minus any advance fees charged by the company, which is usually 1% of the total advance commissions per month.

---

[3] http://kff.org/medicare/issue-brief/medigap-reform-setting-the-context/

So, if we compare the initial commission an agent makes after a sale for each type of plan, we have approximately $450 for a Final Expense Plan and $270 for a Medicare Supplement plan. Most agents would look at these commission averages and assume they should choose Final Expense because it pays more, right?

Residual Commissions

One of the biggest benefits to selling Medicare Supplements is the renewal cycle for residual commissions. While Final Expense commissions pay more the first year after enrollment (up to 110%), the renewal commissions earned in the following years drop significantly to only 7-10% of the premium, depending on the plan. Although Med Supps make smaller commissions the first year (up to 20%), the renewal commission rates stay at that rate for the next five years.

But Med Supp agents don't have to wait until the six-year cycle is up; they can rewrite a client to a new plan at any time, restarting the commission schedule again. Proactive and successful agents shop and compare their Medicare clients' plans every 2-3 years, or whenever rates change, to find their clients opportunities to reduce their rates by switching plans.

There are two main benefits to rewriting your clients every few years: Not only do you help the client find a lower rate, but you can increase your commissions because the client has aged since you first signed them as a client.

	FINAL EXPENSE	MEDICARE SUPPLEMENTS
Average Monthly Premium	$45	$175*
Total Annual Premium	540	1,800
Average Commission Percentage	110%	20%
Total 9 Month Advance	$445	$270
Total 12 Month Commission	$600	$360
Second Year Renewal Percentage	10%	20%
Second Year Renewal Commission	$59	$360
Third Year Renewal Commission	$59	$360
Fourth Year Renewal Commission	$59	$360
Fifth Year Renewal Commission	$59	$400 (newer premium)
Sixth Year Renewal Commission	$59	$400
Total Commission for 6 Years	$889	$2,240

A major obstacle to rewriting Medicare Supplement clients every 2-6 years is their health. It's unfortunate when you hear that your Medigap clients have been diagnosed with cancer or developed complications from diabetes that, when combined with their high blood pressure, make it impossible for them to switch to

* Buying leads in bulk and practicing the tips and scripts in this book will lower the cost of your leads

a cheaper Medigap plan. Of course, not every agent will be able to switch every client every few years.

Selling Medicare Supplements Gives You Freedom Later

Another pro to selling Medicare Supplements is that agents have the freedom to take time off from work whenever they want. Residual commissions from previously sold policies are practically on auto-pilot for six years, whereas if you stop selling Final Expense, your income stream stops.

If you were to suddenly stop selling Medicare Supplements after building a book of clients, it would take 3-6 years for your commissions to evaporate noticeably before having to prospect again for additional clients. Having residual commissions creates a safety net allowing agents time off without worrying about their income abruptly stopping.

Selling Final Expense Gives You Financial Freedom Now

A good justification for selling Final Expense as your primary vertical of insurance is that you get a larger portion of commissions upfront as opposed to waiting 5-6 years to receive it in the form of residuals from your renewals. If you look at it from an investment standpoint, your principal has a better chance of earning more interest if you invest it all upfront, than if you accumulate gradually over six years. Selling Final Expense can potentially be more lucrative for agents than selling Medicare Supplements, especially if commissions are reinvested back into the business to scale growth while keeping policy lapses to a minimum.

2. Sales Environment

When deciding which insurance to sell, it's important to consider the type of clients you'll be working with and the environments you'll be working in. Final Expense clients are typically on a lower income scale than Medicare Supplement clients. This isn't always the case, and it may vary between regions. But you're more likely to come across a Final Expense client on a low to no monthly cost Medicare Advantage plan than on a costlier Medicare Supplement plan.

Lower income clients may lead the Final Expense insurance agent into more urban areas where crime and poverty may be higher unless the agent specifically targets rural areas. Final Expense clients in lower income brackets likely don't have the financial resources to self-fund their funeral, burial, or cremation, whereas Medicare Supplement clients are usually spending upwards of $150 a month or more on their medical insurance and living in rural areas where hospital networks are traditionally sparse.

3. Learning Curve

Another factor agents consider when deciding which insurance to sell is the amount of fundamental knowledge needed to start selling that product. Final Expense life insurance is an easy need to understand because everyone needs a plan to cover all the loose ends when they pass away. Plus, it has a relatively easy application and one-page underwriting/qualification process.

Selling Medicare Supplements is a bit more challenging because it requires the agent to understand the whole Medicare system enough to answer any seniors' questions and to help them find and enroll in a competitive benefits plan. The Medicare system is confusing to seniors (and agents alike) because the government named the 11 standardized Medicare Supplements with letters A through N and also named the different parts of Medicare with letters A through D.

	Medigap Plans									
	A	B	C	D	F	G	K	L	M	N
Part A coinsurance and hospital costs up to an additional 365 days after Medicate benefits are used up	YES	YES	YES	YES	YES	YES	YES	YES	YES	YES
Part B coinsurance or copayment	YES	YES	YES	YES	YES	YES	50%	75%	YES	YES
Blood (first 3 pints)	YES	YES	YES	YES	YES	YES	50%	75%	YES	YES
Part A hospice care coinsurance or copayment	YES	YES	YES	YES	YES	YES	50%	75%	YES	YES
Skilled nursing facility care coinsurance	NO	NO	YES	YES	YES	YES	50%	75%	YES	YES
Part A deductible	NO	YES	YES	YES	YES	YES	50%	75%	50%	YES
Part B deductible	NO	NO	YES	NO	YES	NO	NO	NO	NO	NO
Part B excess charge	NO	NO	NO	NO	YES	YES	NO	NO	NO	NO
Foreign travel exchange (up to plan limits)	NO	NO	80%	80%	80%	80%	NO	NO	80%	80%
Out-of-pocket limit	N/A	N/A	N/A	N/A	N/A	N/A	$4,940	$2,470	N/A	N/A

If Med Supp agents also want to sell Medicare Advantage Plans and/or Part D prescription drug plans, they'll be subject to additional annual certifications by AHIP and the individual companies they contract with.

4. Customer Service

Besides the commission structure, learning curve, and sales environment, the level of customer service is a major difference between selling Final Expense or Medicare Supplements. Life insurance is traditionally considered a one-and-done type of sale because when people buy policies, especially Final Expense whole life plans, they usually intend to keep the coverage for the rest of their life.

Medicare Supplement clients require substantially more service from their agents. These are not the types of plans you set-and-forget because the Medicare system is constantly changing. Proactive Med Supp agents will call their clients periodically to explain any changes in Medicare — which requires the agent to stay up on plan changes and price increases. Most Med Supp agents contact their clients at least once a year to answer any questions and to maintain good relations so other agents can't easily steal the client away. If you're shopping clients' Part D prescription drug plan during Annual Enrollment Period (AEP), then you might contact the client more than once a year. Every three to four years, it's wise to re-shop clients' Medigap coverage to keep their rates low. All of these check-ups mean the Med Supp agent has considerably more customer service to perform compared to the life insurance agent.

The biggest potential customer service issue agents face when selling Final Expense is the unusually high probability of clients missing payments and "lapsing" their policies within the first few years. Final Expense policies cater to seniors who aren't healthy enough to pass a fully underwritten life insurance exam or don't want to deal with the hassle of having a nurse come and take their blood and urine. Due to the "simplified issue" nature of Final Expense life insurance, and the fact that many people seek this policy when they're living on a fixed income after retirement (because they didn't take out a life insurance policy at a younger age when it would have been less expensive), there's a higher chance of clients lapsing their policies and creating a "chargeback" on the agent. Insurance companies may charge back the whole advanced commission or the unearned premium left from the advance. So, if an agent receives a nine-month advance of commission and the client lapses four months into the policy, the company may require all nine months to be returned or just the five months of unearned premium.

That's why a Final Expense agent's customer service efforts are centered around the first year, trying to "stay on the books" to keep the policy from lapsing. After the 13th month, the agent doesn't have to worry about lapses anymore from a commission standpoint. However, due to the high prevalence of lapsing Final Expense policies, it's not uncommon for agents to rewrite clients during the first year or several after that.

If you rewrite a client during the first year of a new policy with the same company, you likely won't see a new commission. If you rewrite the client to a different company, either for the first year or after, you will earn a new commission.

Final Expense agents might see anywhere from 5-20% of their policies lapse depending on how affordable of a plan the agent signed the prospect up for. The amount of customer service and rapport established by the agent play a big role in preventing these lapses. For example, sales that happen over the phone are more likely to lapse than those that result from face-to-face meetings where trust is more easily established. The more an agent stays in touch with his customers, the better chance he might have to rewrite those clients again — and even gain valuable referrals from them — which will boost the Final Expense agent's bottom line.

DIFFERENCES	FINAL EXPENSE	MEDICARE SUPPLEMENTS
COMMISSIONS	HIGHER	LOWER
SALES ENVIRONMENT	LOWER INCOME CLIENTS	MODERATE-HIGHER INCOME CLIENTS
LEARNING CURVE	LESS TO LEARN	MORE TO LEARN
CUSTOMER SERVICE	FIRST YEAR	CONTINUOUS

Now that we looked at the four main differences between the types of insurance, let's take a closer look at the individual types of insurance to get a better understanding of what's involved with selling each.

FINAL EXPENSE

Final expenses range from $2,500 for cremation to more than $15,000 for a traditional funeral and burial. Here's an average breakdown of costs, which may differ based on location:

- Casket: $2,300
- Embalming: $500
- Grave site: $1,000
- Funeral director's services: $1,500
- Obituary: $50-$500
- Funeral service charge for the chapel: $500
- Flowers: $100
- Cost to dig the grave: $600

- Grave liner or outer burial container: $1,000
- Headstone: $1,500

At any budget, one fact remains: the $255 Social Security lump sum for a dependent (or spouse) survivor might not even pay for the obituary and flowers. Instead of leaving their grieving families a legacy of debt, seniors can cover these loose ends with a Final Expense whole life insurance policy.

Why Seniors Need a Final Expense Plan

Seniors typically buy Final Expense life insurance policies because they:

1. Didn't set aside cash earlier in life to pay for their funeral, burial, or cremation expenses — not to mention other expenses that might occur when they pass away, including hospital and doctor bills, unpaid debt obligations, Medicare deductibles/co-pays, or probate costs.
2. Never got life insurance when they were younger and healthier (when premiums would have been considerably less expensive).
3. Relied on a life insurance policy they got through their employer. After they retired, they realized they might:
    a. Lose the plan entirely if it's not "portable,"
    b. Face higher premiums if the company stops subsidizing, or
    c. See their death benefit cut in half for the same or similar premium.

When faced with the monumental task of finding an affordable Final Expense insurance plan, seniors inevitably come across two different types of life insurance.

Two Types of Life Insurance

There are two types of life insurance seniors can consider when planning how to protect their families from funeral and burial costs. The first and least expensive type is term life insurance. As the name suggests, term life insurance policies only cover a fixed period of 15, 20, or even 30 years. After that guaranteed time, the policy ends and the senior has to qualify for another policy at higher rates because they are now older and possibly have more health conditions than when they qualified for the original policy. This type of policy may be unavailable for some seniors because insurance companies often limit the age at which they will sell someone a term life insurance policy — which may restrict a senior's options.

The second type of life insurance a senior might buy is a permanent policy. A permanent life insurance policy will last until the senior passes away if all the premiums are paid on time. Most permanent policies also build cash value that plan owners can access through loans or withdrawals. Because of the extended coverage and cash value, permanent life insurance policies cost considerably more than term life policies.

Within this permanent coverage, there are two major types of Final Expense life insurance: first-day coverage and graded (or modified) policies. A first day coverage policy's death benefit pays out in full immediately, even if the insured passes away within the first year and pays a couple of payments. A graded or modified Final Expense policy generally pays a portion of the death benefit in the first year, increases in the second year, and matures in the third year, at which point the full benefits would be paid if the insured died.

Reasons to Specialize in Final Expense

There are many reasons to specialize in Final Expense insurance. Here are the top five reasons that make this a lucrative insurance vertical to sell:

1. The simple application process only asks about 10 health questions, which is easier for seniors than taking a physical exam and filling out a 20-page application for traditional fully underwritten life insurance plans.

2. Selling this policy is pretty straightforward because the benefits are easy to explain to seniors: If you die, your family gets paid, simple as that.

3. The policy takes less than a week or two to issue, which means fewer buyers are opting out due to buyer's remorse.

4. Commissions are generous, averaging between 100%-120% of the first year's premium.

5. Because baby boomers make up a large subset of the country's population, there's a growing tsunami of them who need permanent policies to cover their final expenses.

Pros Vs. Cons

If we look at the pros versus the cons for selling Final Expense life insurance, the biggest pro is the large commissions, and the biggest con is keeping clients on the books because life insurance is not a necessity for seniors living on fixed incomes struggling Social Security check to Social Security check. Now let's take a look at the complementary senior insurance covered in this book.

Medicare Supplements

What is Medicare?

Agents need to understand the five basic areas of Medicare to effectively sell Medicare Supplements:

Part A covers hospital insurance. Seniors may be required to pay a deductible and/or co-insurance.

Part B covers medical insurance, typically picking up 80% of the bill and leaving seniors to pay the other 20% out-of-pocket.

Part C or Medicare Advantage plans cover Parts A and B, plus some of the gaps those leave uncovered, as well as Part D and possibly some supplemental benefits like dental, vision, or hearing. Seniors on these plans may be subject to co-pays, co-insurance, and deductibles.

Part D covers prescription drug benefits.

Medicare Supplement or Medigap plans cover the costs that Parts A and B don't, for a predictable monthly premium with typically fewer out-of-pocket expenses than Medicare Advantage. Medigap plans have no Part D coverage so seniors are required to buy a separate Part D prescription plan.

A senior turning 65 and enrolling in Medicare has three main options for combining these five components to cover their health care needs:

1. Stay on Original Medicare (Parts A and B) and pay out-of-pocket for the gaps Medicare doesn't cover.

2. Enroll in a Medicare Advantage plan (Part C), which covers Parts A and B, and usually Part D.

3. Enroll in a Medicare Supplement plan that will pay for any costs that Medicare Parts A and B don't cover, and add a separate Part D plan on the side to cover

prescription drug costs costing on average $30-$120 a month.

It's vital that agents understand the fundamental parts of Medicare to be able to answer questions from prospects and clients. Even if you only sell Medicare Supplement plans, you should still know how they compare to Original Medicare and Medicare Advantage plans.

Should I Offer Medicare Advantage (Part C)?

Insurance agents who sell Medicare Supplements have to decide if they should offer Medicare Advantage plans as well. There are extra requirements to sell these plans, including additional certification, continuing education, and marketing rules.

Agents wanting to sell Medicare Advantage plans have to pass annual AHIP certification in addition to individual product certifications with every insurance company they represent. Plus, The Centers for Medicare & Medicaid Services (CMS) sets more rigorous marketing rules for selling Medicare Advantage plans than for Medicare Supplement plans.

Although selling more types of insurance products can make an agent more well-rounded, you won't usually find Medicare Advantage plans sold where Medicare Supplement plans are sold. That's because Medicare Advantage plans are often competitive in urban environments where hospital networks are more condensed, and doctors are more plentiful. In rural areas where networks are more spread out and doctors are fewer and farther between, Medicare Supplement plans are more prevalent because they give seniors greater freedom to go to any hospital.

Seniors might choose a Medicare Supplement over a Medicare Advantage plan if they'd rather pay a predictable monthly premium than hassle with the co-pays, deductibles, co-insurance, or maximum out-of-pocket limits often found in Medicare Advantage plans. One of the biggest reasons seniors might enroll in a Medicare Supplement plan over a Medicare Advantage plan is so they can go to any doctor that accepts Medicare. Conversely, Medicare Advantage plans limit seniors to a certain network, sometimes requiring referrals from a primary care physician to see other doctors. This is particularly evident with seniors who want to see specialists outside of their local area. For instance, if a senior in North Carolina wanted world-class heart care from the Cleveland Clinic, her Medicare Advantage plan probably wouldn't cover it — whereas a Medicare Supplement plan would. This is especially critical for snowbirds or seniors with vacation homes who spend part of the year in another state; they're better served by flexible Med Supps than the network limitations of Medicare Advantage.

Seniors who don't like change might also choose a Medicare Supplement over a Medicare Advantage plan because every year, Medicare Advantage plans could change networks, co-pay amounts, or co-insurance amounts — especially when the federal government cuts funding. Medicare Supplements, on the other hand, include 11 standardized plans with benefits that stay the same every year. This affords seniors a certain amount of predictability knowing their benefits will stay the same as long as they pay the premium.

That's not to say that Medicare Advantage plans aren't as good as Medicare Supplement plans. Medicare Advantage plans are appealing to seniors who would rather have everything wrapped up in one convenient plan instead of keeping track of both a Medicare Supplement plan and a separate Part D plan. Seniors may also choose a Medicare Advantage plan if all of their doctors are accepted in the network, or if they're not worried about co-pays because they don't have a lot of prescriptions.

Should I Offer Prescription Plans (Part D)?

Agents who sell Medicare Supplements also have to decide if they'll offer Part D prescription drug plans to their clients. There are extra requirements to offering these types of plans, just as with Medicare Advantage. There's the hassle of passing the AHIP every year, being under the scrutiny of CMS with every interaction, and having to recertify with each insurance company's plans.

The commissions for Part D plans are negligible — less than $75 per enrollment — and renewals are usually half of that or less. Many agents don't want to jump through the additional hurdles for this low-commission, high-maintenance product.

However, there are three reasons why agents might want to offer Part D plans to their clients:

1. For the commissions (although low, money is money and every little bit counts).
2. To gain a full-service advantage and prevent other agents from wedging between them and their clients when AEP season starts.
3. To gain more referrals.

Since many Med Supp agents don't offer Part D plans, it can give you an edge to help you stand out in a crowded field of insurance agents who all offer the same plans.

How is it Sold? T65 Vs. T67

Another decision Medicare Supplement agents have to make is whether to prospect "T65" seniors who are turning 65 and opting into Medicare plans for the first time, or to prospect "T67" seniors who have already been on their plans for a couple of years and understand a little bit about how Medicare works.

Newer agents might want to start off selling to the T67 crowd because these seniors already understand the Medicare system and may have already experienced rate increases in their Med Supp plans. Plus, commissions come quicker because agents can enroll T67 seniors within a month after helping them apply, whereas agents could wait 3-5 months to initially enroll seniors just turning 65.

The two main reasons agents prospect seniors turning 65 is that this may be a less prospected demographic in your area because of the above reasons. This may help avoid competition, letting you get to senior clients before another agent does. Plus, if you can get these clients when they turn 65 and provide great service, you'll probably keep their business for life.

Medicare Supplement Plan F Vs. G Vs. N

Agents selling Medicare Supplements primarily concern themselves with the three most popular supplements: Plans F, G, and N.

Plan F is known as the gold standard or the Cadillac of supplements. Seniors are only responsible for the monthly premium (which is known as "first dollar coverage.") The rest of their medical bills are paid, provided that Medicare Parts A or B cover the expense.

Plan G is very similar to Plan F in that it covers all of the same things except one: the annual Part B deductible, which is $183 for 2017. After the senior pays that deductible, the plan acts like a Plan F for the rest of the year. The difference in the monthly premium that a senior will pay for Plan F to have the insurance company cover that $183 can be two to three times the amount of the deductible itself. Not only does Plan G cost less on average than Plan F because of this; it also has lower rate increases due to two factors:

- Plan G requires seniors to qualify by answering a series of health history questions, whereas Plan F guarantees acceptance for certain situations (like coming off of Medicaid or group health care). This means fewer claims with Plan G because, theoretically, it covers healthier people.

- Plan G doesn't have to cover the Part B deductible. Because Plan F supplements do cover the Part B deductible, their prices go up whenever the deductible goes up. Plan G requires policyholders to pay the Part B deductible, which is a cost-sharing measure that encourages more frugal medical expenditures by making seniors think twice about unnecessary trips to the doctor if they have to pay out-of-pocket for care.

Because Plan G typically has lower rate increases and lower monthly premiums, it's the wiser choice in most cases. There are exceptions, of course, like in some areas where Plan G rates aren't much cheaper than Plan F.

Medigap Benefits	MEDIGAP PLANS		
	F	G	N
Part A coinsurance and hospital costs up to an additional 365 days after Medicare benefits are used up	YES	YES	YES
Part B coinsurance or copayment	YES	YES	YES
Blood (first 3 pints)	YES	YES	YES
Part A hospice care coinsurance or copayment	YES	YES	YES
Skilled nursing facility care coinsurance	YES	YES	YES
Part A deductible	YES	YES	YES
Part B deductible	YES	NO	NO
Part B excess charge	YES	YES	NO
Foreign travel exchange (up to plan limits)	YES	YES	YES

Plan N is very similar to Plan G; both require seniors to pay the annual Part B deductible of $183. Where Plan N differs from Plan G is that seniors are responsible for a $50 co-pay when they go to the emergency room and a co-insurance co-pay of up to $20 when they see their doctor. The difference in premiums between Plan G and Plan N can be anywhere from $15-$30 or more a month, for an annual savings of $180-$360 with Plan N. On average; Plan N also has lower rate increases — and even more savings — when compared to Plan F.

WHAT ABOUT EXCESS CHARGES?

One feature of Plan N that makes it hard to sell is explaining what "excess charges" are. Excess charges are what a health care provider charges beyond what Medicare will pay. Providers who accept Medicare's payment in its entirety are known as providers who "accept assignment." About 5% of U.S. providers are not willing to accept assignment, and instead, charge more than what Medicare pays. Many seniors never come across these providers at all, because these doctors:

- Are limited to a 9.25% cap they're able to charge beyond what Medicare will pay.
- Must direct bill the client, which may require hiring extra collections personnel.
- Forfeit quicker payments from Medicare because providers that accept assignment get priority.

These hassles make it easier for providers to accept assignment, explaining why most seniors rarely encounter "excess charges." But there is that possibility, so the easiest way to navigate that hurdle is to advise clients to visit Medicare's[4] website and click on the additional search options to find doctors who accept assignment.

In some states, seniors don't have to worry about the possibility of excess charges at all. **Ohio**, **Minnesota**, **Vermont**, **Connecticut**, **Rhode Island**, **Pennsylvania**, and **Massachusetts** have all outlawed the practice, so a Plan N might make even more sense in these states.

---

[4] http://www.medicare.gov/physiciancompare/search.html

Plan F is Going Away in 2020

In April 2015, Congress passed legislation to fix several Medicare issues, mostly known as the "doc-fix" bill. This legislation forbids insurance companies from selling Plan F starting in the year 2020. The theory was that seniors who had first-dollar coverage plans would abuse the benefits without having cost-share measures to restrict unwarranted trips to the doctor for small inflictions like a headache or the flu.

There are two schools of thought when it comes to informing Medicare clients of this change. One approach is to inform clients of the pending change coming in 2020, noting that they can keep Plan F if they want, but there may be potential rate increases on closed-off books of business without new people joining the plan. The other school of thought is that bringing up this legislation may be considered scaremongering, especially if it's used to entice seniors to change Medicare plans.

Agents have to tread a fine line when informing seniors of their choices as 2020 approaches. Because insurance companies aren't entirely transparent on how they calculate rate increases, we can't say for sure whether this change will raise rates or not. The additional benefits of changing from Plan F to Plan G or N are usually apparent, so those should be the main selling points for an agent. Since Plans G and N typically see lower rate increases than Plan F, doubling down on potential "closed book of business" increases won't add any value beyond the usual lower rate increases those plans already enjoy — at least not in the eyes of consumers who don't specialize in Medicare and can't quantify rate increases beyond the fact that they happen.

Note About Military

If you are selling Medicare Supplements, you'll no doubt come across veterans looking for more info on their benefits. This book will not endeavor to explain the differences between TRICARE or VA benefits. Suffice to say, thank these men and women for their service and refer them to someone who has more experience serving veterans.

Reasons to Specialize in Med Supps

There are just as many reasons to specialize in Med Supps as there are for Final Expense. Here are the top five reasons that make this a lucrative insurance vertical to sell:

1. Renewals can eventually compound to very large commissions.
2. Agents can sell this over the phone easier than Final Expense.
3. Due to the continued required amount of service work every year, there's the potential for more referrals.
4. It's easier to sell Medicare Supplements to seniors and then cross-sell them a Final Expense plan with the savings, than it is to sell a Final Expense plan initially and then cross-selling Med Supp.
5. Agents don't have to visit lower income areas as often as a Final Expense agent might.

Pros Vs. Cons

When you commit to selling Medicare Supplements, you're trading the higher commission you would've earned selling Final Expense plans, for the opportunity to amass a book of business that will eventually give you exponential residual commissions. That is the biggest pro of selling Med Supps. The con of selling Medicare Supplements centers around three areas:

1. Cultivating enough trust over the phone to enroll a senior in a plan.
2. The annual need for check-ins (via phone, email, or card).

3. The initial low commissions you make starting out when you don't have that many clients and have to pay for leads

Does It Have to Be *Either* Final Expense *Or* Med Supps?

Some agents looking at these two types of insurance will see obvious differences between commissions, the learning curve it takes to get up-to-speed to sell, the amount of annual service required, and the sales environment. A more experienced agent will not look at these two types of insurance in terms of having to sell one or the other, and may decide instead to sell both. If you're catering to seniors in both instances, why not offer both products? There are other benefits besides the increased amounts of commission from offering both, which we'll discuss more in the cross-selling chapter.

For the agents who are just starting out and wisely focusing on one type of insurance first, the next steps after figuring out which insurance to sell is determining what kind of leads to order and how to prepare to contact and follow up with them. We'll cover this in the next few chapters.

CHAPTER 2: AGENT PREP CHECKLIST: WHAT TO DO BEFORE ORDERING LEADS

Before we get into the different kinds of leads, how to order them, and how to contact them once you receive them, we need to address a few things the agent should have taken care of up to this point. Also we would like to point out that every section will be covered more in-depth on our blog, so be sure to check back regularly for our new informative posts!

1. Licensing

The majority of agents reading this have already passed their state licensing exams. However, if you are lucky enough to find this book before jumping into the insurance industry, the first thing you will want to do is get your insurance license. The best way to find out what is needed to contract for a given state is to visit www.nipr.com.

2. Contracting

There are two questions agents ask themselves when deciding to contract with insurance companies or "seeking appointments" as it is called in the industry. First, should you go captive or independent? A captive agent is bound to only sell one company's products, whether or not those products are the most competitive. An independent agent, on the other hand, contracts with several companies based on which products are most competitive in a geographical area or which ones accept seniors with certain conditions.

The second question agents have to ask themselves is whether they should go through a distribution system — like a field marketing organization (FMO) also known as an independent marketing organization (IMO) — or go directly to insurance companies for their contracts. There are several possible benefits when an agent aligns with an FMO/IMO:

- lead discounts
- non-qualified deferred compensation
- trips and bonuses based on sales performance
- marketing reimbursement

The dark side of contracting, whether you go captive or work with a marketing organization, is the release. Insurance companies rarely allow dual contracts, meaning an agent can't have multiple contracts with the same insurance company through different agencies at the same time. So, if you want to switch your contract for selling a particular company's products from your current FMO to another IMO with better commissions or perks, your current FMO first needs to grant you a release.

If you're a captive agent, applying for a release is basically like handing in your resignation. However, not all companies will allow releases, especially if they don't want agents to take their training secrets to another agency. Where it can get complicated is if you signed a non-compete clause forbidding you to take clients with you when you leave the company.

Getting a release from an FMO is a little different. In this case, you're trying to get a different contract with the same insurance company through another FMO instead of the FMO you're currently using. Some FMO's might make agents wait up to 6 months after writing the last piece of business through them with that particular company before granting a release.

When agents first sign up with an agency or an FMO, they don't always think ahead to consider that they may be forbidden from leaving or switching companies down the road. This is why it's imperative to read your contracts and understand any non-compete or release clauses upfront. If there's no mention of releases, ask the company about it before contracting.

3. Commissions as Earned Vs. Advances

Whether you sell Final Expense, Medicare Supplements, or both, you'll have to decide if you want the first nine months (or even 12 months) of commission paid in advance. The biggest reasons agents want to take advances is because it allows them to:

- have money to live on while they're building their book of business, and
- reinvest more money back into their lead marketing program, compounding client growth.

The two biggest reasons agents wouldn't want to *stay* on advanced commissions after the first few years is because:

- Possible chargebacks hitting them if clients lapse their policies (this is more evident when selling Final Expense) and,
- The insurance company charges interest on the total advanced commissions, reducing an agent's first year commissions (FYC).

It may make sense for an agent to take advances for the first two to three years to support himself (maybe his family) and pay for leads at the same time; but then move over to "as-earned" commissions, if possible.

4. Errors and Omissions Insurance

You need to purchase Errors and Omissions (E&O) insurance before running your leads. Most insurance companies require agents to get E&O insurance. This is the liability insurance agents have to buy before selling insurance themselves. It is a hallmark of professionalism in the industry. This insurance can cost upwards of $450 a year for this coverage. If you offer indexed annuities it may be higher.

5. Continuing Education Requirements

Insurance agents have to recertify for their licenses regularly. The average amount of continuing education required for agents is about 24 hours every other year. It's up to each state to mandate the number of hours, so visit the National Insurance Producer Registry – www.nipr.com – or your state's department of insurance website. Among some of the more popular continuing education providers are Kaplan Financial and WebCE, but most agents will be able to access local training as well for insurance company related continuing education classes. Be sure to check with all the major insurance company offices in your area to see if there are any CE classes coming up.

6. Traditional Applications Vs. E-Apps

Before writing your first application, you need to decide if it's going to be a physical paper application or an electronic e-app. An e-app is usually quicker, with less hassle carrying around and faxing paperwork that could have incomplete fields, which may force the insurance company to drag the application process out. E-apps are designed so the application process can't continue until all required fields are filled out on each page.

As quick and easy as e-apps are, there are times when you might want to use a paper application. If you're setting appointments to see your clients for a face-to-face presentation, you might want to use a traditional application as a qualifying tool while helping the prospect complete the necessary paperwork. Qualifying with a paper application gives the agent an excuse to bring out the application without making the prospect apprehensive that the agent is trying to close a sale. Filling out a tangible application and signing with a pen can also be more personable and comfortable for many people born before the digital age, and can establish a feeling of commitment when they sign their name in ink.

7. Learning Underwriting

Understanding the insurance underwriting process is probably the steepest learning curve for both Final Expense and Medicare Supplement agents. Each company is different in how it qualifies health conditions to accept seniors. The more companies an agent contracts with, the more underwriting processes he has to learn over time.

For example, you'll have to understand which insurance companies accept which existing health conditions, and which medications for those conditions the company may cover. The comparison of health conditions and medications for multiple companies can get complicated quickly, especially if the prospect has been diagnosed with multiple conditions and prescribed multiple medications. One condition may be acceptable, but combine it with another condition and this creates a decline for the prospect.

Your up-line or FMO should have an underwriting resource for you that compares the company's underwriting decisions for multiple common conditions. If they don't, you will have to compile the top companies in the state(s) you work in and look at the most common ailments listed in the presentation chapters for each insurance. All of the conditions and medications accepted by all of the insurance companies in the country would be far too large to include here, but Lead Heroes will be putting together a general underwriting guide for the top companies, so agents have a reference for their underwriting questions.

8. Business Cards

One last thing you'll want to take care of before you start ordering leads and selling insurance is getting some business cards. Handing out your contact info not only makes you accessible to clients and prospects, it also makes you look professional. (At the end of this book, we'll dive deeper into how you can expand your professional brand image online as well.)

When it comes to making business cards, we recommend Vistaprint; it's a very helpful website that easily guides you through the process of creating a business card or brochure, with plenty of ready-made templates. If you look around the internet, you can usually find a promo code for a discount on your first order. We'll post these codes on our site from time to time as we find them, so be sure to check us out when you're ready to order your business cards.

Agents should have all of these preliminary issues cleared up before proceeding to order leads. After all, the last thing an agent wants to do is order leads weeks before he's able to write any of those leads with a company.

9. Quoting Software

This is perhaps one of the more indispensable tools an agent wanting to be successful will need as he meets with his clients (online or in person). Popular quoting software options for agents include CSG Actuarial, Quotit, FEXQuote, and the free option sponsored by Craig Ritter's agency Ritter Insurance Marketing. Options differ in:

- Pricing and packaging ranging from free to over a hundred dollars per month or more, depending on package and add-ons selected.
- Types of insurance quoted, FEXQuote displays quotes for Final Expense life insurance but not for Medicare plans, whereas Quotit, CSG, and RitterIM have both Final Expense and Medicare Supplement plan pricing (some for an extra charge).

- Underwriting information for a given company in relation to a certain ailment.

It's really a no-brainer. If you are boot-strapping with your marketing budget, then go with the Ritter quote engine. If you have some money to spare, then go with a paid version. Of course, you can always stop by the Lead Heroes website to use our free access to some of these quote engines; all you have to do is order a batch of leads once a year and we will give you free access to all of our tools. That, in and of itself, is worth more than the cost of the leads themselves!

10. Customer Relationship Management (CRM) Tool

Agents without a CRM database will find themselves quickly in over their heads. How else are you supposed to keep track of all your leads and your interactions with them? We talk about some options in the chapter, "Staying on Track," but be sure to pick out a CRM up before you order your first batch of leads.

11. Tools for Online and Telesales

Going forward, online screen sharing tools will be utilized more often as baby boomers and seniors alike start plugging into more technological ways of communicating. This tool is used more by Medicare Supplement agents than Final Expense agents, due to the more common nature of how the two types of insurance are sold, Final Expense mostly sold face-to-face and Medicare Supplements sold over the phone. The three top free screen sharing software programs insurance agents use to successfully sell insurance online and over the phone are Join.me, Mikogo, and Zoho. There are other paid providers out there like Citrix GoToMeeting, Screenleap, and Zoom.

Of course, it goes without saying that if you are going to be doing telesales via screen share, you will want a nice almost five-star webcam like Logitech's HD Pro Webcam C920 for $100 ($30 off if you order it off of Amazon). At the end of the day you don't want to come across like a basement troll in a darkly lit room when you finally connect with the prospect to show them:

1. Your license and about you
2. How the plan works
3. What the savings (or costs) are and how the application process works

A nice webcam will go a long way to coming across professionally composed and as an expert in your field.

While you are picking up the webcam, you might as well order a nice headset. VERY IMPORTANT to remember when deciding on a headset, make sure it plugs into the computer via USB and not the stereo jacks. Having the headset (wired or wireless) engage through the USB utilizes the computer's sound card audio system more efficiently than a stereo jack.

If you are going for cordless, we recommend the Logitech Wireless Headset H600 Over-The-Head Design (for $20 on Amazon) which has a nano receiver to plug into a USB port on the computer so you can stand up when you are talking and get more vibrancy and fuller breaths while on the phone making calls.

12. Dedicated Phone Number and Fax

Every agent, whether presenting over the phone or doing face-to-face sales, needs a dedicated phone number for their business. If you think Ms. Jones won't mind the catchy ring tone you have on your phone as opposed to a clear articulate message waiting for prospects/clients when they call you back, then you will have a hard time creating that polished image that makes an agent referable.

What are agents supposed to say on their outgoing message? Here is an example:

"Hello. You've reached ***FIRST & LAST NAME,*** *I am not available at the moment; I am either helping a client or away from desk. Please leave a detailed message with your phone number so I can return your phone call within 24 hours. Have a great day!"*

That's all you need. If you want to add your company you can, but you're better off using just your name so that when the prospect invariably looks up your name and phone number (if you're prospecting), they will see your branded information, website, and hopefully a "welcome" video to put a face with a voice and measure your authenticity and confidence within your voice.

In addition to the phone line with voice mail capability, some online providers will add an additional fax line or make the number **itself** the fax number, allowing agents to fax applications over the internet instead of using up their commissions on postage.

Next we will take a look at the different types of leads available to agents to get in front of prospects, to see if they can help them with finding a Final Expense or Medicare Supplement plan.

CHAPTER 3: TYPES OF LEADS (AND HOW TO ORDER THEM)

First, we compared the pros and cons of selling Final Expense or Medicare Supplements, and then we explained what prep work agents should do before ordering leads. Now, let's talk about the different kinds of leads you can order, and the pros and cons of each.

WHAT IS A LEAD?

Leads are prospective consumers who have either directly or indirectly expressed interest in a product or solution. Just because these people have expressed interest doesn't mean they are necessarily ready to enroll in an insurance plan today; they may be in a different stage of the buying cycle. (We'll dive deeper into the buyer's cycle when we discuss online branding in Part IV of this book).

In this section, we'll classify leads as either cold or warm, which refers to how much interest they've expressed in your service before you try to sell it to them. Did they take action to request info about your solutions, or did you just call them trying to drum up interest? Cold leads are prospects you contact out of the blue who haven't necessarily expressed interest in what you're selling (yet). The warmer a lead is, the more directly they have displayed a desire for what you're selling, which may lead to them requesting more information from you.

- Who are you?
- Why are you calling?
- What company are you with?

- What does the plan cover?
- How much does it cost?
- How do I apply?

With a little effort and sales savvy, cold leads can develop a need for your solution and become warm leads. However, some agents decide to focus on warmer leads so they can spend their time qualifying prospects instead of trying to develop them. A qualified lead has not only expressed the desire for more information or even a quote, but has also answered the health questions necessary to obtain a policy and is happy with the affordability of the solution presented to them. Affordability, to qualified a Final Expense lead, might mean a low monthly premium that *fits* their budget, whereas an affordable Med Supp might be one that *frees up* their budget instead. (We'll talk more about this critical nuance in Part II of this book where we go more in-depth with the sales process).

Once you find leads, whether cold or warm, it's your job as an agent to help answer any questions or concerns they have, to qualify them, and help enroll them in the best plan.

Note About Prospecting Older Generations

Like a Boy Scout helping an old lady across the street or raking a senior's leaves for a service project, so too must an agent act with the utmost patience, kindness, and ethics. Seniors are naturally distrustful due to financial fraud. Don't tarnish the reputation of the insurance agent by putting someone in a plan that isn't suitable or for appropriate reasons. Approach them as you would your own parents/grandparents, patiently answer all their questions (some times more than once), and guide them in their old age through the treacherous landscape of insurance that could easily cost them tens if not hundreds more in dollars per month if they aren't careful selecting a competitive plan with the benefits they are looking for.

Now that we have that out of the way, let's get to the 7 ways an insurance can prospect for leads. There are perhaps more than these 7, but for the most part these are the ones you should focus on. Leave the radio and television commercials for the larger agencies.

7 Ways to Get in Front of Seniors

There are seven main ways to prospect for Final Expense or Medicare Supplement leads. Agents might consider different approaches to different types of leads, depending on:

- How you plan to qualify leads and present solutions — whether in-person locally or on the phone, possibly with seniors out-of-state.
- How much leads **cost** to purchase.
- How much **time** and marketing effort is required to convert leads into clients.
- How much **trust** each method instills within the leads at the time of generation.

Most traditional marketing is interruptive marketing, where you run a TV commercial, a radio ad, or even make a phone call that interrupts whatever the audience or consumer was doing. The audience didn't necessarily ask for that ad, but they're receiving it. For that reason, interruptive marketing lead generation techniques can have an unintended consequence of attracting unqualified leads because this is not a particularly targeted approach.

With permission-based marketing, on the other hand, a prospect has to deliberately take action and request more information. Permission-based marketing can be a superior lead generation tactic that creates higher quality leads when compared to interruptive marketing, but it can also be a more expensive marketing strategy.

Whatever lead generation strategy or lead type you choose, all seven prospecting methods we'll examine below differ when it comes to **TIME** to execute, **COST** to purchase, and the amount of **TRUST** the method instills in the prospect, in addition to the pros and cons with each lead generation method.

Going Door-To-Door

TIME: Long

COST: Low

TRUST: Low

Door-knocking can be a challenge due to possible local solicitation permits. Researching, notifying, and buying solicitation permits is time-consuming. Plus, you also have to buy a data list and a comfortable pair of walking shoes, and pray that rain, snow, or heat don't ruin the day. For a list of quality data vendor options, be sure to stop back by our website,[5] where we will soon have a more in-depth article on the options facing agents when it comes to finding their own data.

One great thing about door-knocking is that there's very little competition — probably because spending all day trudging around and driving up and down streets at the mercy of the weather doesn't exactly sound appealing. For some agents who like to get out and mingle on a nice day, this could be your cup of tea. You

[5] http://www.leadheroes.com/

can certainly develop leads this way, but it would take an incredible amount of time to cultivate enough leads on a weekly basis. This technique can also be draining if the agent is driving across multiple cities door-knocking seniors who fit certain filters. So, for most agents, door-knocking isn't a viable, *dependable* prospecting strategy.

PROS: cheapest, gets you out of the office

CONS: a lot of time prospecting = less time presenting, laborious, cold lead source, interruptive marketing with potential solicitation limitations

Cold Calling

TIME: Long

COST: Low

TRUST: Low

Cold calling is a lead generation tactic where the agent calls a list of prospects with a power-dialer (like CallFire, Mojo, SalesDialers, EVS7 Dolphin Dialer) to find interested people to either present solutions to or set appointments to present at a later date. Cold calling can be a tiring and long process; more than half of the people you call won't answer, and the majority that do answer won't be interested in what you have to say or sell. The goal of cold calling is to catch people interested in either saving money on their Medicare Supplement or getting a plan to spare their family the cost of a burial and other final expenses. It can either be an impulsive interest, or you just caught them at the right time.

Nathan Robinson cold calls seniors with this easy and short script:

"The reason for my call is that I'm helping folks between the ages of 50 and 80 cover 100% of the costs of their funeral and burial expenses with low-cost Final Expense insurance policies."

"Would you like to find out how affordable it would be for you to qualify for these special state-regulated life insurance programs?"

A large obstacle for agents cold calling seniors is that the majority of them are on the Do Not Call (DNC) Registry. Calling seniors on this list can result in thousands of dollars in fines if the agent is caught and prosecuted. This problem is further exacerbated for Medicare Supplement agents because a portion of Medicare enrollees are on a Medicare Advantage plan and unable to switch to a supplement until AEP if their health allows. The DNC Registry, combined with the Medicare Advantage Penetration Rate (MAPR), can limit an agent's list of potential prospects.

CAUTION

This book doesn't discuss potential legal ramifications of cold calling seniors with automatic dialing software. This is another reason why agents may want to consider a different prospecting strategy.

According to the U.S. Census Bureau, there are 45 million seniors age 65 and older — and that number is set to double in 45 years. At least half of them are on the DNC list, which leaves 22.5 million seniors accessible by phone. However, 16.5 million of them may be on a Medicare Advantage plan, so the total Medicare Supplement population that agents can potentially contact is 6 million seniors.

The other obstacle is trying to call a sufficient number of people within a short period. Most agents resort to renting dialing software that allows them to call multiple prospects at a time, which theoretically enables them to talk to more people more quickly than manually dialing. Dialing solutions can cost, on average, $100 a month, with tools to skip voicemail message systems and automatically dial the next number to find prospects who pick up the phone — which can reduce the actual dialing time an agent needs to perform to get in front of a large number of people.

PROS: cheapest, connects agents with more people in less time compared to door-knocking	**CONS:** a lot of time prospecting = less time presenting, laborious, cold lead source, interruptive marketing

TELEMARKETED (TM) LEADS

TIME: Short

COST: Low

TRUST: Low

Telemarketed leads are one step beyond cold calling, because instead of calling prospects yourself, you outsource the process to a company or an assistant that's dedicated to creating these types of leads. By doing the cold calling for you, telemarketing companies begin to qualify prospects by asking if they want to receive more information. Though this can warm up cold leads, telemarketing still stems from interruptive marketing, so the agent will still have to qualify these leads — but this can be a more efficient use of the agent's time than cold calling leads himself.

Because telemarketing companies generate these leads on a mass scale, the agent can focus on selling and forgo:

- Software costs for dialing leads.
- The laboriousness of calling thousands of people each week and getting a lot of 'no's.
- Posting job ads and interviewing telemarketers.
- Training hired telemarketers.
- Managing the telemarketing process.

If you were to buy telemarketed leads from a telemarketing company, each lead might cost about $7-$10 apiece, depending how many you order (many lead providers offer volume discounts).

If you have the available HR capabilities, desire, and time, there's no reason why you can't hire a telemarketer from an online job platform like Upwork, Freelancer, or Craigslist. If you decide to go this route, understand that Upwork, Freelancer, and other online hiring sites are a global marketplace, and some international telemarketing applicants might have thick accents, which may factor into their rates, ranging from $5-$15 an hour. As a general quota, a telemarketer should be able to create two unqualified leads an hour (meaning, leads who express an interest in receiving a quote or more information) and one qualified lead in an hour to an hour and a half (meaning, leads who have not only expressed interest, but have no declinable health conditions and may or may not know their current plan information).

PROS: cheaper than many sources, warmer leads, outsources the laborious task of dialing

CONS: interruptive marketing = tougher lead source, high competition

Direct Mail (DM) Leads

TIME: Long

COST: High

TRUST: Moderate

To execute a direct mail campaign, an agent first orders reply mailer cards to be delivered to a list of prospects. Then recipients who are interested may return the reply mailer weeks later to request more information.

Direct mail can be considered a permission-based marketing technique because interested seniors take the time to fill out the reply card and send it back for more info. This makes direct mail a more qualified lead source than telemarketing.

Most mail houses require minimum orders of at least 1,000-2,000 pieces. But beware: some DM vendors may exclusively serve a single insurance agent/agency in a certain territory, eliminating competition — which is only a good thing if you're that one lucky agent.

Direct mail reply rates differ, depending whether you're selling Final Expense or Medicare Supplements. Final Expense mail gets about a 1% return, on average, which is 10 replies per 1,000 pieces sent out. With Medicare Supplement DM campaigns, the number of returns is slightly higher, at 2-3%. If the average mail drop costs $450 per 1,000, then each Final Expense lead costs $45, and each Medicare Supplement lead costs $15-$22.

The slightly higher return with Med Supp mailers may be misleading because you have to consider the MAPR. More than half of those respondents may be on a Medicare Advantage plan, which means you won't be able to change them over to a Medicare Supplement until AEP, assuming their health qualifies, and they want to pay potentially higher monthly premiums than what their current Medicare Advantage plan charges (it may be nothing).

One pitfall with the standard direct mail reply cards for Final Expense and Medicare Supplements is that they tend to use general and vague wording, like: "You may qualify for a tax-free, state-regulated program that pays for your funeral expenses. You're entitled to receive free information about your eligibility by returning this card today." This nonspecific wording is designed to get the highest number of replies, allowing the agent more chances to meet with more people to qualify leads.

Using more direct, precise wording on a mailer to sell Final Expense or Medicare Supplements may decrease the return rate, but you'll only hear from the most qualified leads who know exactly what they are sending back and requesting information about. When selecting the sales copy for your DM campaign, you have to decide if you want to spend more time contacting more respondents to qualify your prospects, or narrow your focus in the beginning to target more qualified leads.

New agents who need to hone their sales presentation, as well as experienced agents looking to cross-sell more products, may opt for mailers with vague wording so that they can get in front of as many people as possible. Of course, this may mean spending a considerable amount of time qualifying more leads.

In some areas, the DM response rates may be higher or lower than these averages. It's up to each agent to experiment and see what your local average is. You may have to drop 10,000 pieces or more to get a good idea of the average returns.

Agents who sell multiple types of insurance — like life insurance, Medicare Supplements, and Medicare Advantage plans — may have better luck just ordering Medicare leads, because Medicare mailers typically have a higher return, which might get you into more houses to cross-sell Final Expense than the Final

Expense mailer would. A good strategy for agents who cross-sell is to order both types and see which one brings in more sales.

PROS: proof of their request for more info, warmer leads, permissive marketing

CONS: expensive, although leads are warmer they still require some sales effort and education, mail houses may have exclusive territory policies, ambiguous language can attract unqualified leads

Internet Leads

TIME: Short

COST: Higher

TRUST: High

Internet leads come from two main sources: pay-per-click (PPC) ads and organic search results. PPC marketing uses a text or banner ad that entices web traffic to visit a website and fill out a form to have an agent (sometimes multiple agents) contact them back. Besides the possible agent competition when following up with these leads, PPC can be cost-prohibitive, ranging from $30 to $40 or more per lead.

Internet leads from organic search results are people who found your website by typing a query into a search engine browser like Google or Bing, rather than going through an ad. Ultimately, organic search result leads are the best type of leads because the leads find you instead of vice versa – but they come at a great price. To rank in the top three search results takes months, if not years, of refining your website and maintaining your online presence. The average internet marketing firm may charge $1,500-$2,500 or more per month for search engine results they can't even guarantee (beware the ones that do guarantee it). Even if you do invest in this long-term lead generation strategy, you still have one gigantic gatekeeper that can control your lead flow: Google, whose constant algorithm changes make it increasingly difficult to consistently pop up in organic search results.

The great thing about internet leads is that they voluntarily filled out a form and requested info. This isn't an interruptive marketing strategy, which some sales experts would say generates a more qualified, warmer lead. If you're still wondering whether seniors use the internet enough to make the web a valuable lead source for Final Expense and Med Supps, don't forget to read Part IV of the book where we look at other ways to passively cultivate internet leads to supplement your marketing efforts.

PROS: proof of their request for more info, warmer leads, permissive marketing

CONS: very expensive, high competition, potential for fraud makes seniors leery

SEMINAR LEADS

TIME: Long

COST: Highest

TRUST: Higher

Seminar leads can be some of the best leads, next to referrals, because the agent can present to many people at the same time, as opposed to approaching leads one-by-one. This allows agents to see a greater number of people in a shorter period. Unfortunately, it takes time to plan and coordinate, not to mention money to send invitations and to hire support staff to follow up with leads before and after the seminar.

Final Expense seminars are rare, but not impossible. There are some agents who put them together, and for those who get enough people to attend their seminar, this can be a potentially lucrative option.

CAUTION

The rules that CMS institutes for marketing Medicare Advantage and Part D plans seem to change every year, so it's imperative that agents research the current CMS rules and regulations before presenting Medicare plans to the public.

However, Medicare seminars can be a hassle — particularly if an agent is contracted to sell Medicare Advantage and/or Part D prescription drug plans — due to the marketing restrictions CMS institutes for these products. Some agents think that, as long as you don't mention company or plan specifics, it's okay to talk generally about Medicare Advantage and Part D plans.

PROS: easy to appear an expert = trust, multiple presentations in one, leads are more qualified than DM because of time investment to attend, warmer lead, permissive marketing

CONS: very expensive, time-consuming to set up, requires public speaking skill (or at least comfort), may require knowledge of CMS requirements

Referrals

COST: Nothing

TIME: Long

TRUST: Highest

Marketers can spend millions of dollars trying to convince consumers that they need to buy a certain product, but it's much easier for people to trust the recommendation of a trusted friend or family member. Word-of-mouth referrals are the main force in up to 50% of all purchasing decisions, according to global management consulting firm McKinsey & Co.[6]

Referrals are known as the gold standard of leads. To have people coming to you at the recommendation of other satisfied clients, without having to pay for any additional leads — it doesn't get any better than that.

It takes two elements to start obtaining referrals: good customer service and time. For some, referrals start flowing within the first year; for others, they don't come until the agent makes himself referable. Creating a referable brand is about returning phone calls, finding affordable plans that meet prospects' needs, and having a polished online persona.

Later, in Chapter 9 of this guide, we'll go over some of the ways other agents gain referrals, whether actively soliciting them or passively earning them. Whichever way you decide to obtain referrals, this method has the power to bring more highly qualified leads straight to you, more cost-effectively, than most other lead generation tactics combined.

PROS: warmest leads possible = high trust, low to no cost, gold standard

CONS: hard to obtain, takes time to build a referable reputation, need an online foundation to help sell your services

[6] http://www.mckinsey.com/business-functions/marketing-and-sales/our-insights/a-new-way-to-measure-word-of-mouth-marketing

WHERE DO I FIND LEADS?

A quick search on Google will deliver a ton of results for each type of lead, but many agents find themselves wondering which lead vendor to choose. Lead vendors are a dime a dozen, ranging from scam artists to dependable companies that have been around for years.

The first thing you'll want to do when you find a lead vendor is to look online for reviews. You'll find reviews for some lead providers on the popular insurance forum, www.insurance-forums.net, where agents can share their personal experiences with various lead companies. Agents will want to use established lead companies whose current users are willing to vouch for them.

Agents should also be aware that some lead companies won't allow orders from new customers if they only allow one agent/agency per county or zip code. You'll see this more with direct mail lead vendors than any other type of lead provider, so be sure your area isn't spoken for before getting ready to order.

WHICH TYPE OF LEAD IS THE BEST?

TYPE OF LEAD	TIME TO DEVELOP	COST TO DEVELOP	TRUST IT INSPIRES
Door to Door	Long	Low	Low
Cold Calling	Long	Low	Low
TELEMARKETED	**SHORT**	**LOW**	**LOW**
Direct Mail	Long	High	Moderate
PPC Internet	Short	Higher	High
Seminar	Long	Highest	Higher
Referrals	Long	Nothing	Highest

Of the seven ways to prospect for Final Expense or Medicare Supplement leads, not all the above methods make sense for new agents. In reality, no one will door-knock or cold call (at least for very long), and few agents will begin their careers buying expensive internet leads or organizing seminars. Having just started out, before you begin receiving referrals, the best lead options for new agents are direct mail and telemarketed leads.

There is a huge debate within the insurance industry whether Direct Mail (DM) or Telemarketed Leads (TM) leads are better. To summarize the main points of each lead type:

DIRECT MAIL LEADS

- Expensive
- Takes weeks to execute a campaign
- Sometimes a higher quality lead

TELEMARKETED LEADS

- Cheaper than DM
- Can have leads in a couple of days
- Less qualified leads due to the nature of interruptive marketing

It is our opinion that telemarketed leads are better leads for new agents for the following reasons:

1. Inexpensive and quick way to start a marketing campaign
2. More opportunities to approach and present than direct mail (which gives you practice)
3. Direct mail vendors often reserve areas exclusively for other insurance clients

This book focuses on new agents, so from here on out we will address prospecting and selling using telemarketed leads because we believe those give the new agent the most training opportunities possible. However, you will find examples of DM scripts here as well. We recommend that new agents get in front of as many people as possible at the beginning of their career so they can perfect their presentation. It's only after you get more proficient in presenting that you should start to mix in other types of leads.

Of course, if you are more proficient in presenting, and your budget is more accommodating, we recommend doing ***both*** direct mail and telemarketed leads for these reasons:

- You can order and start working telemarketed leads before your direct mail leads begin arriving, which can optimize your activity levels.
- Many seniors are on the DNC Registry and cannot be telemarketed; mailing them is an easy way to get around that.

Different types of prospecting are more effective in some areas than others; working both lead types can help you determine which lead type works best for you in your area. Just remember: It takes about 100 or more leads of each type to figure out your efficiency. One lead order won't cut it; you need larger numbers to see how the averages play out.

How Many Leads Should I Buy?

This is perhaps the most common question we hear from new agents. To figure out how many leads you need, you first need to figure out the average policy's commission. In the first chapter, we determined that Medicare Supplements pay an average commission of $360 for the first year's commission, and Final Expense plans pay about $600.

Once you know the average commission, work backward from your desired monthly income to figure out how many policies you need to sell to meet your goal. For our example, we will use a desired monthly income of $4,100 to give the agent an annual income of almost $50,000. To earn $4,100 a month, a Final Expense agent would have to sell about seven policies a month, a little less than two policies a week. Medicare Supplement agents need to sell 12 policies a month, or almost three policies a week.

But what about advances and the cost of leads? Before we can tackle those two concerns, we must figure out how many leads an agent needs to buy to make a sale. Without that number, you'll be spinning your wheels trying to decide how many leads to order.

The consensus among the collaborators for this book was that a new agent should sell around two plans per 10 direct mail leads for Final Expense, and one plan per 10 direct mail leads for Medicare Supplements (assuming a moderate Medicare Advantage Penetration Rate or MAPR). It takes more telemarketed leads than direct mail leads to make a sale, due to the nature of the marketing methods — direct mail being permission-based and telemarketing being interruptive. Which means it takes new agents approximately 25%-50% more telemarketed leads than direct mail leads to close the same number of sales. This means an agent using telemarketed leads would have to order 12 leads to close one Medicare Supplement sale, and an agent selling Final Expense could sell 1 out of 10 telemarketed leads.

Your results may vary, of course, depending on your sales region and experience. We're using conservative estimates as an example for new agents. Keep in mind: This doesn't take into consideration cross-selling or following up with leads that either aren't ready to buy or can't qualify for a plan when you first contact them.

As we said earlier, telemarketed leads cost between $7-$10 (depending on how many you buy in bulk). If a new agent sells one Final Expense plan from 10 leads, the cost is around $100 for those leads. A new Medicare Supplement agent would spend a little more for the same amount to get one sale.

10 Final Expense TM leads = $100 for one sale

12 Med Supp TM leads = $120 for one sale

In Chapter 1, we said the average commission a Final Expense agent earns is about $600 per policy. After taking into consideration the cost of leads minus the commissions ($600-$100) an agent has a net profit of $500. This means a Final Expense agent would need to order about 85 leads for the month to make $50,000 a year.

Also in Chapter 1, we said the average commission for a Medicare Supplement agent is about $360 for the first year. After taking into consideration the cost of leads minus the commissions ($360-$120) an agent has a net profit of $240. This means a Medicare Supplement agent would need to order about 200 leads a month to make $50,000 a year.

To summarize:

- It takes up to 25%-50% more TM leads than DM leads to close the same number of sales (though results may vary).
- A Final Expense policy pays $600 in commission, and a Med Supp policy pays $360 in commission.
- A new agent can sell one Final Expense plan per 10 leads or one Med Supp plan per 12 leads.
- 10 Final Expense leads cost $100 and 12 Medicare Supplement telemarketed leads cost $120.
- An agent earns a net profit of $500 for selling one Final Expense plan per 10 TM leads, or $240 for selling one Med Supp TM lead per 12 leads.
- It takes 85 Final Expense TM leads a month (or 1,020 TM leads a year) to sell $50,000 a year, whereas it takes 200 Med Supp TM leads a month (or 2,400 leads a year) to sell $50,000 a year.

	FINAL EXPENSE	MEDICARE SUPPLEMENTS
Average Monthly Premium	$45	$175*
Total Annual Premium	$540	$1,800
Average Commission Percentage	110%	20%
Total 12 Month Commission	$600	$360
Number of Leads to Make a Sale	1 OUT OF 10	1 OUT OF 12
Cost of TM Leads (non-bulk buy)	$100	$120
Profit After Lead Costs	$500	$240
Number of Policies to Earn $50,000 yr.	100	209

Looking at this, why wouldn't agents choose Final Expense as their specialty? Let's see what it takes to hit that annual income goal in the second year, and if you remember our little chart from the first chapter, you will know where I am going with this.

For Final Expense, residuals are less than 10%, so for the second year, a Final Expense agent would need to earn $45,000 plus residuals from the first year to earn the desired $50,000 annual income. (As a side note, we never recommend that Final Expense agents rely on residuals as commission, but look at it as a bonus.) To sell $45,000 worth of policies in the second year, the Final Expense agent needs to order 918 leads, as opposed to 1,020 leads from the first year.

Taking residuals into consideration for Medicare Supplements, this is where it gets good for agents. In the second year, Med Supp agents theoretically don't have to order any leads to earn the same

---

* Buying leads in bulk and practicing the tips and scripts in this book will lower the cost of your leads

commissions they did in the first year because Med Supp agents enjoy the same commission for years 1-6 if clients stay on the books.

So agents must ask themselves:

- Would you rather get more commissions upfront, but have to work roughly the same amount of leads year to year to maintain the same income?
- Or would you rather earn a lower commission and work way more leads than a Final Expense agent to enjoy the same income level, but enjoy the same commission renewals for the next five years? This doesn't even take into consideration what happens if the Medicare Supplement agent continues to work leads and add clients in the second year.

That's a pretty tough dilemma. Later in this book, we'll take a look at how agents keep and cross-sell their current clients to decrease the amount of leads that need to be ordered regardless of either insurance type they help seniors enroll in.

What Are Filters?

Before you can order leads, you need to know which filters to utilize, so you don't lose money prospecting to people who don't fit the description of your average Final Expense or Med Supp client. Lead vendors use various demographic filters to help agents hone in on the perfect client subset. Advertising to people who don't fit the mold is a waste of money and time, so it's imperative that agents understand which filters or qualifiers to identify to their lead vendor when ordering leads.

The most common filters to use when ordering insurance leads are:

1. Age

2. Income (though not an entirely accurate filter, because it's hard to assess the true income level for a household or individual)

3. Geographic area (usually by zip code or county)

There's one more filter commonly used by Medicare Supplement agents, and that is the Medicare Advantage Penetration Rate (MAPR). You can find the MAPR on the CMS website,[7] and some lead vendors also have MAPR search filters on their websites.

Final Expense agents may want their filters to look something like this:

1. Age: 50-80. Some agents trying to cross-sell Medicare to lower their lead costs will narrow the range to 65-80.

2. Income: $15,000-$45,000. At lower incomes, you'll get people who are on Medicaid or can't afford the plan; and at higher income levels, you'll find people who usually have their affairs in order or can afford to self-fund their Final Expenses.

3. Area: It depends whether you're doing face-to-face appointments locally or selling over the phone.

Medicare Supplement agents may want their filters to look more like this:

1. Age: 65-75. Some agents don't mind the extra time it takes to prospect to people just turning 65 and going on Medicare for the first time, while others focus on older T67 seniors as we discussed in Chapter 1.

---

[7] https://www.cms.gov/Research-Statistics-Data-and-Systems/Statistics-Trends-and-Reports/MCRAdvPartDEnrolData/MA-State-County-Penetration.html

2. Income: $25,000 and up. People at all income levels want to save money on their Medicare Supplement plans.
3. Area: Again, depends whether you're doing face-to-face appointments locally or selling over the phone.

Some agents will tweak these filters even more. We suggest starting with these filters above, and experimenting with your targets as you gain more experience. Also, tweaking these filters like the age settings can dramatically reduce the number of leads you may get in a given area.

Now that you know the different types of leads in addition to the appropriate filters to use when ordering your leads, you need to think about what to say and how you will enroll seniors (face-to-face or over the phone) when you start receiving the leads you've ordered.

PART II.
THE INSURANCE SALES PROCESS: HOW LEADS BECOME CLIENTS

CHAPTER 4: INITIALLY CONTACTING YOUR LEADS

In this chapter we will explore:

- How to initially contact your leads once you order them
- Whether you should qualify leads before setting appointments
- What obstacles you must overcome when selling over the phone
- How to handle objections you might encounter when initially contacting leads

When we asked our collaborators how they approach their telemarketed leads, we found two distinct patterns. The first clear pattern was that agents either (A) call up their leads to set appointments, or (B) call to qualify leads over the phone and then present options at that time or at a later call-back time after researching quotes. Agents were fairly evenly split between these two methods. The second pattern showed that even though there were equal numbers of agents calling to set an appointment or calling to present over the phone, the preference for one or the other was split according to the type of insurance the agent was selling.

More of our Final Expense collaborators called to set an appointment than to present solely over the phone. Conversely, our Medicare Supplement collaborators primarily sold over the phone, with few calling to set face-to-face appointments.

The third option collaborators chose, which was the minority option, was to call and qualify leads over the phone before setting an appointment to visit them in person. Most of the collaborators that qualify their leads before setting appointments sell Final Expense, rather than Medicare Supplements.

Two Approaches to Contacting Your Leads

Agents contemplating ordering leads should decide how they'll approach these prospects when the leads are delivered. There are two ways to approach leads: going to their home and door-knocking them, or calling them up to set an appointment first. Of course, if you only sell over the phone, you have just one option: calling them and presenting over the phone.

Otherwise, there are many opinions on which approach is the most effective: cold door-knocking leads or calling first to set appointments. Door-knocking may lead to higher sales percentages for beginners, because when you show up on prospects' doorsteps, it's harder for them to say no to someone asking for five minutes of their time. The problem is you have to route your leads, incur wear-and-tear on your car driving all over town, and pay for gas to visit these leads, hoping they'll be home.

Based on the feedback of our collaborators, we recommend that new agents call to set an appointment first — or at least try. Our collaborators agree that if you can't get ahold of leads beforehand, then go ahead and door-knock if the drive isn't too far. But generally, it's better to call telemarketed leads before showing up because:

- Calling is quicker than knocking; you save time and money by not traveling to door-knock leads who aren't home or available.
- Even if you find leads at home, some seniors may consider it rude to drop by unexpectedly — potentially delaying or derailing the sales cycle.

- Because calling can be quicker, you can streamline the sales cycle from the start, bringing in commissions sooner.

Todd R. King notes how he handles hard-to-reach leads:

> *"If I have that much trouble reaching them by phone, I'll probably be door knocking the lead."*

Calling Leads to Set Appointments

Setting an appointment will go more smoothly if the agent knows what he's going to say beforehand, as opposed to winging it. If the agent picks up the phone without a plan, he may not cover the four ingredients critical to a successful appointment setting call:

1. **Identity:** The first element of a successful call is simply stating who you are when you get ahold of the lead. By introducing yourself to the prospect, you're telling them you are a legitimate professional following up on their request for more information.

2. **Company:** Telling the prospect which company you work for has two effects. First, similar to the identity variable, is that being upfront with your company affiliation lends legitimacy to the call. Suddenly you're not an unknown caller; you have a more concrete identity. Conveying your company name can also be great if you have a solid online brand because the majority of seniors who have computers are probably looking up your number to determine if they should answer when you call.

3. **Reason:** Giving the reason for the call reminds prospects of their desire for a solution to a certain problem, which is why they responded to the telemarketer to become a lead in the first place. Whether you're calling for Final Expense or Medicare Supplements, relaying the reason helps jog the prospects' memory about the initial call where they

expressed interest, reminding them that there is a latent problem that needs to be addressed. That problem is either the need to protect their loved ones from inheriting the debt of their final expenses, or overpaying for their Medicare Supplement plan.

4. **Timing:** There are two parts to the timing variable: letting prospects know you won't take up much of their time, and narrowing down a time when they're available for you to drop by and give them the information they requested. By limiting the appointment to 15-20 minutes, you assure prospects that you don't intend to camp out all day until they buy.

   Limiting the appointment also gives the impression that you are busy helping others with this same concern, which may stimulate the "herd effect" in prospects. Sure, the appointment may take longer than that, but that depends on the prospect.

If the prospect is interested in what you have to say, which is the "information" you told them you would bring, you can then move into the quoting phase which is technically not part of the initial appointment time. A true appointment length for an interested prospect could be 45 minutes to an hour, depending how much time is spent warming up the client with small talk, how long it takes to present, and the time required to take an application.

If the agent understands and hits all four points, his chances of setting an appointment increase. It's important to note that the point of the call isn't to sell the prospect the solution; the agent's job is to first sell the appointment, *then* sell the solution once you get in the door.

Here's how some of our collaborators call to set appointments with telemarketed leads:

Frank Bahr greets the leads he calls with:

> *"Hello, PROSPECT,*
>
> *You recently spoke with one of our associates, NAME, and shared with us that you had some questions about funeral insurance. We would be glad to answer all of your questions. AGENT, the person that handles that for your area, will be available Thursday for a brief 15-minute visit. Would 9 a.m. or 1 p.m. work better for you?"*

Ron Wiza likes to qualify his leads' needs by ending on an open-ended question designed to elicit a reason why they're looking for a plan:

> *"Hi, my name is AGENT. The reason for my call is because you had requested information from us regarding burial or Final Expense insurance. I'm the person who handles that. How can I help you?"*

Tom Massey calls Medicare Supplement leads he intends to meet with by saying:

> *"Hi Betty, this is Tom. You requested information about lowering your Medicare Supplement premium. I'll be in town tomorrow to see if you qualify...would you prefer morning or afternoon?"*

Carlos Guillen calls his leads by saying:

> *"Yes, PROSPECT?*
>
> *Hi, this is AGENT from COMPANY calling you regarding the information you requested about Burial Plans available in your area. Yes, you just talked to one of our representatives and I need to verify a couple of things with you, PROSPECT. We have your address as...Is that correct? How young are you, PROSPECT? Perfect..."*

Brandon Webster starts out all calls asking if the client is there.

"Hi, PROSPECT, it's AGENT returning the call from yesterday. I am calling because I am the local burial insurance expert in your area. Just so we are correct, you mentioned to my staff that your hobby is fishing, correct? Okay great. What I would like to do now is see how I can help. I am the local agent and what I do is set a time for us to meet and spend 20 minutes together to go over all of your insurance options and see if we can find a plan that makes sense and is affordable to you. I will be in your area tomorrow. I can either stop by at 10:15 or 1 p.m. Which is better? Great. Now before we go, let me just confirm some information."

Jeff Cornelius calls Medicare Supplement telemarketed leads up initially by saying:

"Mary, this is Jeff with Georgia Medicare Solutions. Recently you talked to someone from our office and you indicated you to them you were interested in saving money on your Medicare Supplement, and I am calling to help you figure that out."

Justin Bilyj calls Medicare Supplement prospects and says:

"Hi, Prospect? My name is Justin, you recently spoke to my assistant yesterday/a few days ago/last week, to see if you qualify for a reduced rate on your Medicare Supplement plan. You mentioned you were with COMPANY and you were paying (amount), is that correct?"

Mike Smith calls direct mail leads by saying:

"Hello, Mr. Smith? (Pause) Mr. Smith, this is AGENT over here in CITY. I'm just trying to get back to you. I received the card that you filled out (short pause) that you mailed back to us, looking for information on state-regulated Final Expense burial plans. Some of them also have living benefits."

I toss the living benefits in there because that perks their interest, and they almost never stop me unless it's to ask what that is. I'm referring to the terminal illness rider that almost all plans have, but agents seldom mention. I have a way of pitching it so they can really see the value in it.

"I just wanted to confirm some information here so I know what to make available to you. What you do with the information is up to you, of course. You're in CITY as well, I see. In terms of your health, any cancer or heart problems in the last 2-5 years — just so I know what information to make available to you? So you're in decent shape, right?"

I use the words "make available to you" and "what you do with the info is up to you." At this point, they still feel as if I'm just going to get them information, all the while bringing down walls.

"Mr. Smith, I'm going to be in CITY on Tuesday visiting with about 10—15 people who requested the same information as you. It takes around 10—15 minutes to get you the information. I typically don't have much more time than that because I'm seeing so many folks. Do mornings or afternoons work best to make that info available to you?"

Instead of just saying it'll take 10-15 minutes, by also saying that I'm seeing 10-15 others already, I don't have a lot of time, and it will only take 10-15 minutes, they'll realize a few things: they know I'm busy, they know I won't be there long, and they know other people do this ... then I book the appointment.

Todd R. King calls Medicare Supplement telemarketed leads initially by saying:

"Hi, PROSPECT, this is AGENT with COMPANY. I'm calling you concerning your Medicare and a recent phone call you received about your Medicare Supplement and the possibility of saving some money without changing your benefits."

The more elements you add to your initial call, whether questions or statements, increase the chances of meeting resistance from the lead. It's much easier to solve the prospect's problems when you have their full, undivided attention in person, rather than trying to cover everything on the initial call — especially if you're new and not sure what to say in response to resistance.

Glen Shelton reminds new agents:

> *"When I'm on the phone to set an appointment, that is the ONLY thing I do: set the appointment.* ***Once*** *I am in the house, I will do more qualifying."*

To Qualify or Not to Qualify? That Is the Question.

For some agents, simply calling to set an appointment is not effective enough. More experienced agents might qualify a lead before setting the appointment. There are two reasons why agents would want to qualify the lead before setting the appointment:

1. They want to maximize their time
2. While minimizing their expenses.

Jason McKenzie believes it's better to just focus on setting the appointment, and then visit the lead to further qualify them:

> *"On the phone I'll ask if they have had any major health changes in the last 2 years or since they had their last policy. I try to keep over the phone qualifying to a minimum to avoid hang ups."*

Jacob Anderson calls Medicare Supplement leads and gets the ball rolling on qualifying the lead to keep the conversation going:

> *"Hello, PROSPECT, I was calling back concerning your conversation the other day, in regards to the rate increases on your Medicare Supplement. Have you got a moment we can discuss the options in getting your rate lowered while keeping the same plan?*

You have Plan F, correct?"

Qualifying the lead — regarding health, interest or, in the case of Final Expense, budget — before setting the appointment allows an agent to spend more time with more qualified prospects who have a greater chance of being able to buy.

Ron Van Duesen, because he presents over the phone, will first begin qualifying the lead by seeing what kind of Medicare plan the lead is on:

"I verify that they have a Med Supp (because some have Medicare Advantage). Then I ask who they are with currently."

If an agent has "more money than time" — meaning, he has built up his book of business and is earning a good income off of it — then this would be a permissible practice. If the agent has "more time than money" — meaning, he is new and has few clients — then he should set as many appointments as possible and try to qualify leads in person.

However, two reasons why agents might *not* want to qualify first is that they could possibly lose the opportunity to cross-sell the lead once they meet, or they could potentially pass up an opportunity to earn referrals. A Medicare Supplement lead's health may not qualify for a Medicare Supplement policy, but chances are the agent can still find a Final Expense company that would take them. Of course, if the agent doesn't cross-sell, then qualifying leads beforehand might help him focus on qualified prospects, not spend time on tire-kickers.

Going On Appointments

Green agents usually have three questions before going to a lead's house:

1. What to wear
2. What to bring

3. What to say when they get to the door.

An agent shouldn't be under-dressed or over-dressed. It's important to give the impression that you are a professional, so don't dress in sneakers, shorts, Hawaiian shirts, or t-shirts. On the other hand, you don't want to come across as an overly-serious salesman, so drop the suit and flashy tie. The happy medium for field work is a pair of pressed slacks (or a skirt), some nice (comfortable) shoes, a blue or white button-up shirt (or blouse), or neutral colored polo. By dressing in a relaxed, professional way and not sticking out for being either under- or over-dressed, you have a better chance of not rubbing someone the wrong way.

When visiting prospects, it's wise for agents not to bring a ton of materials. You'll want to narrow your selection to three or four of the top companies in that area; bring a brochure for each company (if they have one), underwriting or medication lists, and applications. The last thing you want to do is bring an overwhelming stack of papers or materials for every company. Keeping the paperwork to a minimum will help reduce the intimidation factor, so the prospect doesn't get nervous when meeting you for the first time. Traveling light gives the prospect two impressions: First, that you aren't lugging a heavy briefcase to their doorstep to show them every company's products in the state. Secondly, whether your materials are neatly organized in a small folder or on a clipboard, it gives the impression that you are professional enough to prepare the minimum amount of paperwork needed to get the job done, and you understand the area well enough to know how to narrow down the products most relevant to the prospect.

The last item we recommend that agents bring to appointments is a nametag. You can go to any office supply store and buy a 3x4 clear plastic cardholder you can wear as a lanyard or clip to your shirt. After creating the ID, just print it (laminating it will make it last longer) and slip it into the clear name tag holder. Having an identification tag will make you look both official and professional, which helps inspire a level of trust.

When you arrive for the appointment, try to park on the street, rather than in their driveway, to avoid blocking anyone in and later interrupting your presentation. Get out of your car with a smile on your face, as if you're assuming that the prospect is already watching you from the window. Paint the best possible first impression by smiling and standing up straight.

Knock on the lead's door with a friendly tap — as opposed to boisterous banging — to show that you come with good intentions. When they answer the door, introduce yourself and your company and remind them you're there to drop off the information they requested. Wipe your feet, motion toward the door and ask politely, "May I come in?" The majority of the time, they'll let you right in for the pre-scheduled meeting.

After the lead welcomes you inside, the best place to have a conversation is in the kitchen or at the dining room table. This helps minimize any distractions from the television, which may impede your ability to keep the conversation on track and your schedule on time. If the only available sitting area is near a TV, politely ask them to turn it off so you can have their undivided attention, reminding them that you don't intend to take up much time.

On the way into the house, agents often strike up conversation to build rapport and make the lead more comfortable. The most important small-talk topics revolve around C.O.R.E., which stands for **C**ommunity, **O**ccupation, **R**elatives, and **E**xtracurricular activities. Look around the house, compliment them on the cleanliness, and look for any items that fit into one of those topics. If you see tons of family pictures on the wall, a huge plant collection, a pair of fireman's boots in the corner, a cabinet full of trophies, or prized catches mounted on the wall, ask prospects to open up about themselves through these items to build rapport and trust. This helps reduce any concerns that the prospect is meeting with an unfriendly insurance agent only there to sell them a plan and get a commission. The more prospects open up to talking about themselves and what's important to them, the greater the chances of having an open dialogue about their problems and how to best solve them with the products you're presenting. Initially building rapport and trust with leads by getting them to talk about themselves can also serve the agent long after the sale. Being friendly, sincere, genuine, and memorable in the beginning helps build a long-term relationship that will not only keep their business on the books and away from other agents, but also make the agent more referable over time because they've made a good impression and continued to build upon that with the client.

Qualify Then Present

Let's back up a bit. Is it possible to sell prospects completely over the phone without even having to travel to their home to meet and present to them? The answer is yes. That's one of the top benefits of selling insurance: the ability to sell it from the comfort of your own home. Unfortunately, selling entirely over the phone can be harder than face-to-face appointments because a lot of trust is built through human-to-human contact that contains elements of subconscious interaction that help people form impressions to help them judge who is genuine, honest, and professional.

Human interaction and communication happen in five ways:

1. Gestures
2. Expressions
3. Mannerisms
4. Tone
5. Tempo

The only elements a prospect gets to use in a phone conversation to decipher the truth in what the insurance agent is saying are the last two: tone and tempo. People say so much more with gestures, expressions, and mannerisms in addition to their tone and tempo, so selling on the phone potentially limits the amount of rapport you can build with a prospect.

There are three main strategies that allow agents to build more trust when presenting over the phone:

1. Sending mail or emails that contain the information you're conveying to them in the form of product or company brochures, applications, or info about you and your company.
2. Inviting the prospect to an online web conference call with screen share capabilities where they can see what's on your computer screen as you go through plan information, testimonials, licensing, and quotes.
3. Not pressuring leads into making a decision on the first call but taking the time to walk them through the process. You can attempt to close the sale, but only after alleviating any concerns they may have.

Here's how some of our collaborators call up their leads and immediately start qualifying them to determine which solution to present:

Tom Massey is an agent who qualifies and presents over the phone:

> *"I explain that I represent over 15 of the main Medicare Supplement companies and they all underwrite differently. I need to know what medications they take and what major health conditions they've been treated for in the past three years so I can see how much money I can save them for the exact coverage they have now."*

Robin Penrod qualifies a Med Supp lead's interest or "need" upfront before qualifying the health:

"I ask if they are interested in moving forward if I can find a lower premium. I then ask basic questions, "Do you smoke, use oxygen, any surgeries or hospitalization in last two years?"

I will then run a quote and let them know, based on the basic information I have, it looks like they may qualify for a better rate. I then ask if there are any concerns that we need to address before moving forward. I let them know that if there is something going on with their health, if I know upfront I can probably help; if it comes out during underwriting, it may be too late."

Debbie Majher, not wanting to waste any time, presents the budget aspect of the sale (the potential savings) using the objection takeaway technique of qualifying the health:

"Do you know what you are paying now? The best premium I have in your area is $_______. That would be a savings of $_______. How about if we see if you qualify medically so you can receive the savings?"

Jeff Cornelius qualifies Med Supp leads by first verifying the company and then the date of birth, followed by their zip code to run a quote:

"PROSPECT, I see that you are with INSURANCE COMPANY with a Plan F, is that correct? There are few companies in your area that may save you money while keeping the same coverage. Now, all I need to know is your date of birth and whether you have used tobacco in the last few years to get us started saving you money."

Justin Bilyj qualifies a Medicare Supplement prospect:

"I have your zip code as (number), and that you are (number of years) young, is that correct?" "Do you smoke by any chance?" "Lastly are you in good health or do you take any medications?"

"Now the majority of seniors are on a Plan F as in Frank, is that the same plan you have?"

Objections

In Final Expense and Medicare Supplement sales, there are two times when you'll likely encounter objections: when initially contacting the lead, and when you are closing the sale or asking for the application (their enrollment). Objections for Final Expense and Medicare Supplements revolve around four main concerns:

1. Confusion, often in the beginning when initially contacting the lead.
2. Trust, which usually shows up twice: the first time an agent calls and again when they are closing.
3. Budget, which agents are more likely to encounter for Final Expense than Medicare Supplements.
4. Value, which comes up during the initial call and closing time.

1. Confusion

Examples of objections that revolve around confusion include: "I didn't understand what the call was about," "I never asked for a call," "I don't remember getting a call," and "I didn't know this was about insurance."

These responses happen for one of three reasons:

- The phone call didn't stand out compared to what was going on in their life that day.
- The agent took too long to call back, and the senior has since forgotten the conversation.
- The lead creation script was too vague.

The key to dealing with this objection is to remind leads about any security questions that a telemarketing company may use to help jog their memory of the initial call, and to assure them that you're the agent who was supposed to contact them about their concern. These questions can be as simple as a favorite color or hobby. This is a very useful technique when it comes to lead creation and prospecting.

The other way to deal with this objection is to apologize simply for any confusion and proceed with asking them a question about the problem that your solution fixes. Final Expense agents might ask leads if they have a plan that takes care of their loved ones when it comes to paying for their Final Expenses, while Medicare Supplement agents may ask leads if they've gotten their latest rate increase on their supplement or if they think they're overpaying for their supplement. Some agents automatically assume the senior is paying too much for their supplement, and just proceed with the presentation, expecting that any true objections will surface sooner or later. Here are a couple of examples:

Jeff Erb's response to confused Med Supp prospects reiterates the benefits of switching supplements as a way of overcoming their objection: "I didn't know this was for insurance."

I say, "Well, ma'am, we were asking if you would be interested in saving money on your Medicare Supplement."

Nathan Robinson's response to confused leads:

"I give them the name of the telemarketer who gave me their information and what was said. If they still say no, I then apologize to them, and then I ask them if they have the money saved to pay for at least a $7,000 burial ceremony. If they refuse to talk about the issue, I send them my business card and a card in the mail."

2. TRUST

Examples of objections that revolve around trust are: "Mail me some information," "Who are you?" "What company are you with?" "I need to talk to my child/friend/spouse before making a decision," or, "I want to talk to a local agent."

Justin Bilyj's response to "who are you?":

> *"I have to admit I found this off the forums and I have been using it since. I say, "Oh, I apologize. That's a great question. I am not with any one insurance company. There are over 25 companies offering the same exact plan you have now, same benefits, same doctors, only they charge a different price. My job is to help my clients find the best plan their health will allow them to qualify for, so they don't overpay for the same plan and customer service they can get elsewhere."*
>
> *"Are you on a Plan F?"*

Todd R. King responds to the objection, "mail me some information," by saying:

> *"Without knowing a few things about you, I would have to send boxes and boxes of stuff in order to get you ALL of the info you need. It will only take me about 10 minutes with you and then I can get you the specific information you'll need. Is tomorrow at TIME a good time for you?"*

Ron Wiza responds to seniors asking for something to be mailed by saying:

> *"I'm not sure what I would mail you, that's the purpose of me coming to see you. I still need to determine which plans and options you best qualify for. It only takes a few minutes to go over that. Are you a morning or afternoon person? 9 or 11?"*

Joseph Smith responds to the Med Supp prospect's objection, "I want to talk to..." by saying:

"I am glad you want to involve someone else with the decision. Do you feel it is important to ask your child/friend if you should save money? What do you think they will say if they knew you would save $XXX per month for the same exact coverage?"

Mike Shure responds to Final Expense leads' requests for more information to be mailed to them by saying:

"The information we have to mail is generic and just describes the 25+ carriers in our network. If you give me a few minutes we can get you quotes because I know that's what you really need to make a decision, and I'll be happy to send that along with any other information you might need."

Chris Fonner's response to a Medigap prospect's concern or objection, "I want to talk to a local agent" is:

For this one I just say, "Sir, that is not a problem, but let's start by making sure you will qualify first. Do you have a computer?" And I just go from there, and try to get them on a webinar.

These objections happen because prospects lack the information they need to make a decision, and they worry you might not be giving them the whole picture because you receive a commission for selling them a plan. The best way to deal with any objections based on trust is to:

- Let prospects know who you are, either by using an ID, having your insurance license visible, or taking them through a screen share presentation to show them pictures of your family or other clients in addition to your state insurance license.

- Convey personal experiences that humanize you and let prospects know you understand, and can relate to, their situation and concern.

- Send them a video, email, or letter showing the solution to their problem and who you are.
- Get them to acknowledge their priorities, aside from the lack of trust, to see if your solution outweighs their concern.
- Utilize the "herd principle" and tell them their concern isn't uncommon; your other clients also had the same concern before they became your clients, while explaining the reasons your clients were able to look past that concern.

Remember, trust is the hardest objection to overcome, and without it, sales are rarely made. That's also why it's important to have a proactive online brand, so when these issues do come up, prospects can search and see for themselves why they have no reason to worry, especially if you (through your website or the other methods mentioned above) clearly describe plan info, address common problems prospects may have, display your licenses and experience, and share testimonials from other clients.

3. BUDGET

Budgetary objections come up more in Final Expense sales than in Medicare Supplement sales, because agents selling Final Expense are *selling* prospects another bill, whereas agents selling Medicare Supplements are usually *saving* prospects on a bill they already pay.

Frank Bahr responds to budgetary concerns this way:

> *"Most of my clients are on a fixed income, that is why we start small with something affordable. Your family would definitely appreciate whatever you can do. What is it you need to think about? Usually that means you are concerned about the cost, is that right?"*

Medicare Supplement agents selling to people turning 65 (T65) and going on Medicare will come across the budget objection when comparing the cost of low- to no-cost Medicare Advantage plans with seemingly more expensive Medigap plans.

Remember, agents cannot sell Medicare Advantage plans to telemarketed leads because of CMS marketing regulations. However, without going into company or plan specifics, an agent can compare the potential out-of-pocket costs of a Medicare Advantage plan against a Medicare Supplement plan. While making this comparison, agents can remind leads of the "advantages" of Medicare Supplements:

- No network restrictions for doctors or hospitals.
- More stability than Medicare Advantage — where doctors may leave networks, co-pays and covered medicines may change, and plans may be discontinued.
- More predictable out-of-pocket costs than the co-pays, co-insurances, and possible deductibles associated with Medicare Advantage.

If, after comparing the differences between these types of plans, the senior still wants to go with Medicare Advantage because of affordability concerns with Med Supps, then you may not be able to overcome this objection. At this point, the agent has three options:

1. Tell the senior, "I cannot help you with a Medicare Advantage plan. If you find that the Medicare Advantage plan is not for you, and you want to look at your Medicare Supplement options down the road, feel free to contact me." Leave your card, and head to your next appointment.

2. Tell the senior you cannot help with a Medicare Advantage plan, and attempt to cross-sell them a Final Expense plan instead.

3. Partner up with another agent who does sell Medicare Advantage, who can help your leads. Give the senior that agent's contact info or business card, and explain, "Due to the restrictive rules on how agents can contact seniors for Medicare Advantage plans, you'll have to call him for more information; he can't call you first, but he will be able to help you if you reach out."

In the next chapter, where we talk about presenting, you'll see three different ways to ascertain the budget of a Final Expense prospect — or the savings potential of a Medicare Supplement prospect — to avoid this objection altogether.

4. Value

After trust, value is the second hardest objection to overcome. Whereas budgetary objections just question whether prospects can *afford* the cost of a plan, their determination of a plan's *value* depends on how important and beneficial they deem the solution. They wonder: Is it worth the hassle of switching plans or changing providers from what I currently have? The most common value objections an agent will hear include: "I am happy with my current plan/company/agent," "I like my current company; they pay all the bills," (for Medicare Supplement plan sales), or frankly, "I am not interested."

Jason McKenzie responds to objections like, "I'm happy with my company," with:

"I understand that you're happy with the company, but probably not with the last rate increase you got from them. I also write a lot of said company and like them as well, however, I have a lot of clients that are very unhappy about the last rate increase. So what

I have done for them is found another A-rated company with the same Plan F/G and requalified them at a much lower rate."

Ed Murphy, finding out that leads aren't interested because they have another plan:

"I try to find what kind of life insurance plan they have and give an honest evaluation of it. About 80% have a good policy, the rest I try to save them money or get them into a permanent plan because many are with term policies that will end up eventually lapsing, possibly before they pass away."

Todd Graves double checks with Final Expense prospects to make sure they aren't leaving their family with a bill for their final expenses by asking:

"Can your loved ones afford to pay for your funeral out of their pockets when you pass? Or would you rather leave a legacy and not the burden of a huge bill by taking care of your final expenses for pennies on the dollar?"

Joseph Smith educates Medicare Supplement leads who say their plans pay well this way:

"I am happy your plan pays your bills, because federal and state laws mandate that your Medicare Supplement policy must pay the expenses it is required to pay. It pays well because it is supposed to pay, not because they like you. As long as you stay with the same alphabet letter plan, it will pay exactly the same. Precisely the same."

He then reminds prospects of the potential savings and attempts to proceed to taking application.

Brandon Webster asks the lead that isn't interested:

"If I told you could have all of your final expenses covered for less than your cable bill, would that make sense?"

Then, to remind the lead of one's obligations regarding final expenses, he adds:

"We find the money for things that aren't necessary, yet forget the things that are extremely important."

You can overcome value objections one of three ways: wedging between the prospect's current company or agent by providing better service, increasing their benefits for the same cost they're already paying (for Final Expense), or lowering the cost of what they are already paying, (whether it's a Final Expense plan or Medicare Supplement).

Final Thoughts on Overcoming Objections

It's important to understand that objections should be handled with care; agents shouldn't just bulldoze over objections as if the senior's concerns don't matter. Agents have to remember that not everyone will need or want a Final Expense plan or cheaper Medicare Supplement. It's the job of the agent to ask questions to see if there are concerns or problems he can provide a solution to. If there aren't, that's not a problem. If you find yourself trying to fit everyone into a solution and getting angry when someone doesn't like the solution you propose, then step back and remember two things:

1. A lead isn't a guaranteed sale; it's a chance to talk to someone and see if they have a concern with which you can help. If they don't have a problem you can fix, simply file them into the pipeline to follow up with later, and politely move on.

2. No single lead should anger an agent; if it does, the agent simply doesn't have enough appointments set or leads coming in. A busy agent won't care if some leads aren't a fit, he expects it knowing it's part of the business and focuses on the other leads he can help. Expecting every

single one to buy every time is a recipe for discouragement.

Another tactic you can take if you're encountering a lot of objections, or the same types of objections repeatedly, is to design your presentation so it answers the common objections you're hearing before prospects have a chance to utter them. If you keep hearing a common objection from leads, take it upon yourself to look more closely at how you're calling or closing, and see if there are any patterns you may be able to adjust that could possibly prevent objections from happening.

Now that we talked about some of the ways agents can contact seniors regarding their Final Expense or Medicare Supplement, and looked at some ways agents deal with concerns and stalls, we can move on to looking at some more tips when calling and following up with these leads.

CHAPTER 5: TIPS FOR FOLLOWING UP WITH LEADS: HOW TO CONTACT AND REENGAGE UNRESPONSIVE PROSPECTS

Whichever lead source you use, there's always an unfortunate aspect of prospecting: not all of your leads will give you the time of day, and even if they do, they won't all buy. Here are eight tips to maximize your response rates, reengage unresponsive leads, and help you get the most value out of your marketing budget by optimizing the potential of each prospect.

1. Call Right Away

This is the most important factor in getting ahold of your leads. You have to understand that a lead's effectiveness will decrease over time after it's created. The best time to contact a lead is within 48 hours, or the memory of the initial telemarketing call begins to fade. It doesn't mean their need changes; it just means you have a better chance of engaging them in conversation about their needs if they remember requesting more info on Final Expense or Medicare Supplement plans.

2. Call at Different Times

It's important not to limit yourself to a specific time or a certain day to call your leads. Some seniors may still be working, so if you don't get ahold of leads during your morning call session, calling again in the late afternoon can help you contact more of the hard-to-reach leads.

Robin Penrod calls at various times:

> *"I initially will run through my leads about 10-15 times, different days, different times of day, nights and weekends. If I haven't gotten ahold of them by then and they haven't called me to ask*

why I am calling them, they will then go into a master list of leads. I generally go back in three months. If I do make contact, I refresh their memory and let them know I have been trying to reach out and help. I generally try to make a joke, "Wow, you are a busy lady!" Many times they will let me know they still work, have been out of town, etc., but it breaks the ice and opens the door for conversation."

In the morning, we recommend calling no earlier than 9 a.m. The best time to start calling is around 10 a.m.; at this point, most prospects have been awake for some time and finished their morning routines. Agents can call all the way until lunch time, pausing around noon. Then you can start calling again after 2 p.m. until 6:30 p.m. or whenever your appointment slots are filled up for the next couple of days.

Matt Mungia, MBA, outlines his persistent formula to contacting leads at different times:

"Six to eight phone calls at different times of the day to contact unresponsive leads. When I finally get them on the phone, I let them know I have been trying to reach them and it's important that I get this information to them. Then I ask them if tomorrow around a certain time is good or if another time is better."

For incredibly hard-to-reach leads, try calling on Saturday. If at this point you still cannot get ahold of the lead, you can also try door-knocking the lead if it's in close enough in proximity. For a closer look at how successful agents organize their day around making calls, refer to Chapter 10: Staying on Track.

3. Create a Pipeline Lead List

Learning to recycle leads who don't buy the first time around can be critical to an agent's long-term success. Due to life and health changes and rate increases, cold leads may become more receptive to your solutions over time. A pipeline lead is simply a lead that is filed away for contact at a later date. It's important to build a list of pipeline leads that you or your appointment-setting assistant can follow up with, **to minimize lead generation expenses by extracting more value from previously purchased leads**.

Jeff Erb explains that when it comes to following up with pipeline leads:

> *I repeat to them the scenario that prevented them from buying at that time: "Mrs. PROSPECT, my name is AGENT, and I spoke to you about Medicare Supplement insurance back in MONTH. Unfortunately, you were getting ready to have shoulder surgery when we spoke and you had to postpone things until now. How is your shoulder doing?"*
>
> *I make sure I put detailed notes as to why they are not buying for this purpose.*

Some people either aren't ready because they don't have enough information to feel comfortable making a decision, or they have a temporary health condition that may prevent them from gaining coverage.

Expect that some leads are in different parts of the sales cycle, and utilize a pipeline to funnel these people through the process until they are ready to have a conversation or enroll in a plan.

Here are some ways our collaborators approach their pipeline leads:

John Smith approaches pipeline leads by assuming they haven't taken care of their priority yet:

> *"Hello PROSPECT, not too long ago you and I spoke about the state regulated programs to assist you with your final expenses. You told me that you hadn't yet taken care of that. I'm going to be in your area tomorrow evening. I can stop by for about 10 minutes to go over the information with you. Does 5:30 or 7 p.m. work best for you?"*

Ron Van Deusen approaches leads that weren't ready to enroll due to health reasons:

> *"Hi PROSPECT, this is AGENT. You and I had met and reviewed some options regarding life insurance a few weeks ago, and I just wanted to touch base to see if the timing is better to get you on a plan to pay for your final expenses so your family doesn't have to?"*

Garrett Ball says to hard-to-reach leads:

> *"You requested the information but we haven't been able to catch up with you by phone. I wanted to make sure we didn't drop the ball on this."*

Jeff Cornelius says to the lead after calling 3-5 times:

> *"PROSPECT, this is AGENT with COMPANY. A couple of weeks ago you had expressed interest to someone in my office about saving money on your Medicare Supplement and I am calling to help you get that information and save you money. It will only take about five minutes to determine if you qualify for a lower rate. If I could have your birthdate, that will get us started."*

Todd Graves describes his follow-up strategy. He tries to reach leads:

> *Every day for first week then every two or three days, until I get them or get a no. When I reach them I say:*

> *"I see you took the initiative and requested I contact you immediately. My understanding is you're looking for a way not be a big financial burden on your loved ones and you want to learn how to pay for final expenses for pennies on the dollar using a Final Expense policy. Before we get in-depth on the how, tell me about your health..."*

Most agents aren't contracted with every company, which possibly limits coverage for rarer health conditions the agent comes across. It is perfectly okay to tell the prospect that you will research their conditions and come back to them to let them know what you find regarding coverage.

Ron Wiza following up with a pipeline lead over possible health conditions that made it tough to qualify initially:

> *"Hi PROSPECT, this is AGENT. You and I had met and reviewed some options regarding life insurance a few weeks ago. I know at the time we had some issues with your health due to underwriting requirements. However, I've been doing some homework and have some options that I think we should look at. I have some time tomorrow at 4, or would Wednesday morning be better for you?"*

If you follow up too late and find the lead has already purchased a plan from another agent, there's no harm in trying to deliver more value for the senior's premium dollar.

Mike Shure tries to at least beat the other agent's rate to salvage a lead:

> *"Remind them of the original inquiry. If they already bought from another agent, I say, "If we had a better plan with more benefits at a cheaper rate, wouldn't you at least like hear what we have to offer?"*

4. Take Notes

It's wise to take notes on every call you have with a lead. If you have assistants who make calls, qualify, and/or set appointments, they should also be required to take notes. A few things you'll want to include are any mentions of:

- Family members
- Friends

- Hobbies or other recreational activities
- Work or volunteer commitments
- Plan, company, or competing agent info

Todd R. King tells pipeline leads:

> *"Hi PROSPECT, this is AGENT with COMPANY. We spoke briefly a couple of months ago and you asked me to call you back. By the way, how is (the husband, dog, son/daughter) doing?"*
>
> *The agent should have made some notes during the first contact.*

Writing down notes and keeping them handy will help jog your memory of previous conversations with senior prospects. These reminders can be useful when you follow up to see if leads are ready to enroll, and it demonstrates that you paid attention and cared enough to remember some personal details that have nothing to do with taking an application.

5. Leave a Voicemail

Some agents feel compelled to leave a voicemail, while others forgo leaving messages and rely on the curiosity of the lead to call back. We recommend leaving a message for several reasons:

- Other professionals leave voicemails when they call — accountants, realtors, doctors, attorneys, plumbers, etc.
- Leaving a message puts the ball in the leads' court, which can qualify their interest if they take the initiative to call back.

Loran Marmes varies up the times he calls and when he leaves messages:

> *"I call up to eight times, all at different times of the day, different days. Sometimes I leave a message, sometimes I don't. If they*

> *finally answer, I begin the conversation as though they were a brand new lead."*

Some agents would rather get prospects to answer when the phone rings, as opposed to leaving messages that could give them a reason to screen future calls. However, tricking leads to call you back by not leaving a message might confirm their suspicions that whoever's calling is trying to catch them off-guard — even if that's not true. Seniors are taught to be suspicious of people trying to take advantage of them, especially when it comes to financial matters like insurance and health care. By leaving a message, you can show them you're a legitimate professional who wants to help them.

If you cannot get ahold of leads after leaving several messages and possibly door-knocking if they live close-by, then put them into the pipeline list of leads to call in another few weeks or months, hoping they experience some change in the meantime that will motivate them to call you back — or at least answer your next call.

6. Utilize Multiple Modes of Communication

Nathan Robinson explains his process for following up with pipeline leads:

> *"I have access to a computer system that electronically sends emails every month through my Independent Marketing Organization to everyone on my list who has an email. These emails remind the prospect who you are, and the email always ends with my contact information.*
>
> *I also send in the mail educational literature about Final Expense articles from the internet, newspapers, and magazines. After a month, if the customer does not call me, I then pick up the phone and call them. I ask them if they have received my emails and literature that I've sent them in the mail. I also go over the Final Expense market with them at the current time and different issues*

that are arising in the marketplace. I don't pick up the phone and then just ask them for the sale."

Besides calling early and contacting often, agents should utilize as many avenues as possible to get ahold of leads. Some prospects who aren't ready to buy may need multiple contacts over time; this enables the agent to build brand awareness and trust incrementally.

Emailing *and* calling are more effective than calling or emailing alone. Sending a card or a letter is another way to increase brand awareness and trust, adding a personal touch that's increasingly rare in this digital age. Utilizing different forms of communications allows the senior to utilize different senses to build an impression. The more senses utilized, the faster the senior can form an opinion to base their decision on.

Joseph Smith explains the different types of communication he uses to get ahold of his leads:

"I begin calling at 10 a.m. EST until lunch. Follow-ups in early afternoon and another dialing session around 4 p.m. EST. I utilize text, email, and phone to contact my leads."

Texting can be tricky; you don't want to haphazardly text seniors who might be on limited texting plans, adding extra costs to their phone bills. But if you cannot get ahold of the prospect through other methods, you might as well try texting to provide the information the lead requested.

7. Show Them You Care

Denise Rangel shows leads that what matters most is their health, especially if they haven't gotten a plan yet:

"I will try as long as I can to still get in contact with them. I tell them how lucky they are that their health has not changed, because for many seniors it does, and if they would agree, that this is

something that they probably need to go ahead and take care of so as not to burden their children at the time when it is needed."

Tom Massey describes his long-term strategy for following up with pipeline leads:

"I'll try every other day for the first week, then twice a week for a few weeks, then once a month. After a month, I'll try phoning and door-knocking. I'll keep trying for years. I've had sales 10 years after receiving a lead, and sometimes you just never catch them. I just tell them that they had requested the information recently and I was here to see if they're able to qualify."

Jason Eichmiller likes to interject humor into the follow-up process to stand out and put the prospect at ease:

"Lots of phone calls. When I get them, I joke that they were probably called by 17,000 life insurance companies. They laugh...and relax. Not many agents have a sense of humor over the phone.

Then I say, "You probably already bought life insurance, right?" If they say yes, I learn about the policy. If they say no, I ask why and figure out if I can do what the last 17,000 people couldn't."

Each agent needs to differentiate himself from the next agent contacting seniors about their Medicare or life insurance plan. Showing seniors how much you care about them, their generation, and their ability to either save money (on a Medicare Supplement) or spend money wisely (with a Final Expense plan) can give you an edge over competitors. It must be genuine, or you might come across as a scheming salesman who will say and do anything to make the sale.

As an agent, you can show seniors you care by:

- Showing a genuine interest in them, their interests, and their priorities.

- Not pushing or pressuring them to buy, but taking the time to find out what's standing in their way of buying.
- Allowing them time and space to think over the options if, after attempting to overcome their concerns or objections, they still do not buy.
- Attempting to interject humor to defuse any pressure to buy.
- Never giving up on trying to reach them.

8. Cultivate Your Online Brand

This is a very important tip in the 21st Century. More than half of all consumers look up info on the web before making a purchasing decision, whether it's to:

- look up info on the agent
- verify the agent's company
- research the company whose plan was recommended to them by the agent
- look up the phone number when the agent calls initially

Having an online brand that answers the prospects' questions and solves their problems, while introducing yourself and your experience as an agent (testimonials help), is paramount to maximizing your marketing dollars.

There's not one agent reading this that doesn't look up reviews online before buying a product or service. Don't let unsure prospects escape your sales funnel, wasting what you have spent on leads, because they can't find anything online that speaks to your expertise. Commit to creating an effective online brand by putting into practice the principles and techniques outlined later in Part IV of this book. Doing so will increase the amount of trust a lead will develop when they inevitably look you up online. Until then, be sure to cultivate a pipeline list of leads and develop a solid strategy for following up with hard-to-reach ones.

CHAPTER 6: HOW TO CLOSE LEADS BY QUALIFYING, PRESENTING & DEALING WITH OBJECTIONS

This chapter is split into two sections: one for presenting Final Expense life insurance plans, and the other half for presenting Medicare Supplements. We split up this chapter to help readers understand the different sales dynamics with each type of insurance: selling prospects an additional monthly bill to fund a plan to pay for their final expenses versus saving prospects money on an existing monthly bill for their Medigap plans. Because of this inherent difference, agents use different approaches to qualify leads and present solutions for each type of insurance — which is another reason why we divided this chapter in half.

Each half-chapter is divided into three sections about qualifying prospects in terms of their **HEALTH, NEED,** and **BUDGET,** followed by common objections and sprinkled with other insights about each sales process. These areas are key because if an agent can successfully:

- Verify that a prospect **NEEDS** the solution you're presenting,
- Confirm that the prospect's **HEALTH** conditions are accepted by the plan you're recommending, and
- Illustrate that the proposed solution fits (or benefits) the prospect's **BUDGET** …

… all while building trust, overcoming objections, and demonstrating value, then the agent will likely end up taking an application and making a client out of the prospect.

These sections are organized to help agents understand the various elements of these two types of sales processes that need to come together before closing a lead. It is important to note that the order of these sections isn't set in stone; each type of insurance sale may follow a different order for some agents. It isn't uncommon to find Final Expense agents qualifying a lead's budget before they qualify the health, while some Med Supp agents may qualify the lead's health before even visiting the lead to assess budget and need.

The hardest thing for an agent to qualify is the need. Getting seniors to admit that they *need* a solution is a lot tougher than getting them to share their health background or say what they can afford. Whether selling Final Expense or Medicare Supplements, closing a lead ultimately hinges on the agent's ability to educate the prospect about plan options while cultivating enough trust and credibility that the senior feels comfortable taking the agent's recommendation. (For ideas on cultivating credibility from the start, please refer back to previous chapters on initially contacting leads, following up with leads, and later on, building your online brand.)

Keep in mind that the insurance sales process is not cut-and-dried. You shouldn't think of the qualification process as a gate that prospects have to get through before advancing to the presentation stage where they get to see their quotes and plan options. In reality, it's an iterative cycle where qualification and presentation happen in tandem as you educate prospects about their options.

To qualify a prospect's need for Final Expense, for example, you may need to provide education about the various types of life insurance coverage. Maybe you qualify their budget as you present multiple quotes, and then use the health qualification questions to close the sale. Highly experienced agents can transition seamlessly between asking qualifying questions, overcoming obstacles, and presenting plan options in a way that feels more like education than sales, because all throughout the process, they're building rapport and cultivating trust by showing genuine care for each prospect's well-being.

CHAPTER 6A: HOW TO CLOSE FINAL EXPENSE LEADS BY QUALIFYING, PRESENTING & DEALING WITH OBJECTIONS

QUALIFY NEED

There are two main ways to qualify prospects' need when selling Final Expense life insurance plans:

1. Present the three traditional reasons why people buy life insurance and let them pick one.
2. Ask them what they had in mind when they agreed to have someone call them back or visit them about covering the cost of their funeral, burial, or cremation.

The three traditional reasons why people buy Final Expense life insurance plans are:

1. Because they don't have a plan to cover the costs they'll leave behind when they die.
2. Because they have a plan but they're not sure if their plan is the best price or enough coverage.
3. Because they have (at least some of) their final expenses taken care, but they want more coverage so they can leave a small legacy to their favorite child(ren), church, or charity.

Ron Wiza qualifies Final Expense leads in person by saying:

> *"When folks respond to this inquiry, it's usually for one of three reasons:*
>
> *(1) They realize that they don't have any protection in place now and they want to make sure that when they do pass, there will be*

money available to help relieve the financial burden for their family and loved ones.

(2) They have coverage but they're not sure exactly what they have or if it's enough coverage.

(3) They have adequate coverage but would like to purchase a little bit more so that they can leave a special gift for a grandchild, or to their church or their favorite charity.

Of the three, where would you fit in? Is there anyone who would be financially impacted by your death? On a scale of 1 to 10, how important is it to have your final expenses taken care of in case of your death?"

After prospects have indicated their reason for meeting, the agent can ask four additional questions that can paint a complete picture regarding their need for a Final Expense plan:

A. Who their beneficiary is. Whether the beneficiary is financially prepared to pay for their final expenses (if the lead already has a plan in place, this question is unnecessary)

B. How much experience prospects (or their families) have had paying for someone else's final expenses (if the lead already has a plan in place, this question is also unnecessary)

C. How they'd like their body disposed of: traditional burial or cremation

D. If there's anyone else who will need a little help (survivor income) for whatever reason (debt, loss of spouse's Social Security checks, other final expenses not considered) when they pass away.

Let's see how some of the collaborators qualify their prospects' needs for a Final Expense plan:

Matt Mungia, MBA, identifies their last wishes to ascertain their need and budget:

> *"Do you want a full burial or a cremation?" "Who do you want your beneficiary to be?"*

Mike Shure recommends to:

> *"Get the beneficiary names to mention how the plan benefits that specific family member."*

Jason Eichmiller qualifies a lead's need by asking them what happens to them without a plan:

> *"Tell me about your family."*
>
> *(then I show them pictures of my kids).*
>
> *"What happens when you die?"*
>
> *I shut up and listen. If they are short winded I have to lead them,*
>
> *"Who's going to bury you?" "What will your family do?" "How will they afford to bury you?"*

Lawrence Malone dives in to qualify the lead's personal experiences to see if they can relate to the hardship of having to pay for someone's final expenses:

> *"Have you ever had assisted in paying for a loved one's funeral?*
>
> *"If yes, who? Oh wow, so they didn't have ANY life insurance? That had to have been a tough pill to swallow, right? Is there any reason why you haven't purchased any life insurance until now?"*
>
> *(assuming the sell)*

"So if you passed today without life insurance, who will be the person who will have to take care of all your arrangements and be in charge of coming up with the money to pay for it all? Are they in a position right now to do these things?"

"So you don't want BENEFICIARY to have to go through what you did when (whoever died) died, right?"

Denise Rangel builds rapport by being genuine and forthcoming about her own experiences:

"Ask them if they have ever been responsible for paying for someone's funeral, where the family had to gather money from several individuals. Or if they have seen families with a jar at the local stores with a story, trying to collect money for a funeral.

I explain that as a young family with three small children, my husband and I were expected to contribute money for a funeral for a family member and it was very hard for us."

After — or, more likely, *as* — you qualify the need, you begin to educate the lead. Before you present any Final Expense options (which may seem, to prospects, more expensive than the life insurance ads they've seen on television), you'll need to explain the different types of insurance. As you detail what differentiates Final Expense policies from the ones they've seen on TV, you begin building value into the solution.

Todd Graves explains Final Expense policies in terms of immediate death benefit:

"PROSPECT, Final Expense polices pay out the death benefit, no matter how long you've been paying on it. Whether you paid one premium or multiple, it's reliable and immediately available when you pass so your loved ones don't have to worry about what assets they're going to have to sell fast, at less than value, in order to pay for your final expenses."

Educate the prospect on the two different types of insurance: term life insurance and permanent life insurance, like whole life. Whereas a term life policy will eventually expire, possibly before the senior passes away, a whole life policy will last until the senior dies. When explaining this to prospects, stress the point that the best policy to pay for final expenses is a permanent one.

Next, take the prospect a little deeper into the complicated world of insurance. Discuss the two types of coverage or death benefits available through a permanent life insurance policy: immediate (or first day) coverage and graded (or modified) coverage. Explain the differences in coverage, that an immediate death benefit pays out as soon the policy is purchased, whereas a graded death benefit pays out a portion of the death benefit the first year (usually 30%) and increases the second year (usually to 70%), until the third year policy anniversary when the death benefit would pay out its entire face amount.

Carlos Guillen talks about the benefits of a Final Expense policy along with the differences in coverage and types:

> *"I will use a sheet where I explain that whole life insurance is permanent; it never changes, rates never increase, benefit never decreases and stays with you the whole way. Then I will explain the differences between term and permanent life insurance coverage."*

Ron Wiza breaks down the types of insurance and coverage together:

> *"I give a short visual presentation of 'Term vs. Guaranteed Issue vs. Whole Life.' The reason is: I believe the clients see this stuff on the television and in the mail and have questions about it. So I bring it up and explain the differences and how they work and why whole life is best for people on fixed incomes who want to take care of their own final expenses."*

After laying this groundwork, you can educate prospects on the three guarantees of a Final Expense policy:

1. Monthly payment will never change.
2. Death benefit will never decrease.
3. Plan will never cancel, as long as they pay the premium.

Lawrence Malone explains the benefits of a Final Expense plan this way:

> *"What we always suggest for people in your situation is whole life. These plans are regulated by the state of STATE. They are simplified issue, which means you don't have to take any medical exams; you just answer a few health questions and we typically can get you coverage from the first day."*
>
> *"Unlike the plans you might see on the television, the coverage will never expire or cancel regardless of your age and health. Once you get covered, then the policy is guaranteed to pay out as long as you pay your premiums. And your premiums will also never increase."*

Jason Eichmiller explains how he talks about the benefits of a Final Expense policy:

> *"Most of the people I talk with tell* **me** *what the benefits are. We talk about safe and secure programs that are around forever, even if they live to be 120, where the payment never goes up and the death benefit never goes down. We've already established (emotionally) what a burden it would be on their loved ones. Then it's just up to the agent to find a policy that's affordable."*

Glen Shelton explains the benefits of a Final Expense policy like this:

> *"This one is going to sound silly but I SWEAR it always seemed to click for seniors when explaining Final Expense life insurance*

(whole life insurance). I would either draw a bucket on a blank piece of paper or bring a picture of a bucket with me. I would explain that if the bucket was full, it would be worth their death benefit (ex. $10,000). If they only made 10 premium payments of $50 a month before they passed away, their loved ones would still receive the full $10,000 (at this point circling the $10,000 at the top of the bucket and drawing an arrow with the $50 going into the bucket only filling up approximately 5% of the bucket), yet their loved ones receiving the entire $10,000 TAX-FREE."

I say, "Even if you don't save up the money, your loved ones still receive the benefit. Not to mention after years of paying into this policy, it builds cash value with interest (the savings account that these folks never had)! Here's the catch: not everyone qualifies, and in order to qualify, I have to see if I can get your health qualified. Let me ask you a few health questions ..."

You should also explain additional supplementary benefits of a Final Expense plan, like how the policy builds cash value that seniors can access in emergency situations, and how the death benefit bypasses probate and pays out tax-free to the beneficiary. (This is where the lines between educating and presenting may blur).

Tamara Sasso explains Final Expense insurance and supplemental benefits like this:

"I explain that it is a whole life policy, it lasts the rest of their life, that it starts day-one coverage (unless health issues are major). I let them know there is a cash value in the policy, that the company will pay their family out with a tax-free check, and anything else that needs to be said with each client."

Matt Mungia, MBA, explains how he utilizes the brochure to relay benefits:

> *"I use the brochure from a carrier that I am appointed with. I use that brochure in EVERY appointment since most all my plans work the same way."*

It's important to recap all of the benefits with the biggest benefit of all, which is each prospect's main reason or "why" they asked for more information about their final expenses. Remind prospects of this reason to remind them of their priorities, which will help solidify the benefits and education you've gone over with them.

Michael Smith discusses the importance of tying up all of the benefits with the main reason why the prospect is getting the plan in the first place:

> *"Benefits are directly related to their WHY. You can talk benefits all day long, but if it doesn't address their WHY, then you're not getting anywhere. That's why TIE BACKS to their WHY are so important; they remind the prospect of their priorities and desire to leave a positive legacy."*

Mary Dioguardi wraps up with the main purpose and benefit of a plan, to leave a positive legacy:

> *I tell them, "This is the last thing that your kids and family will remember about you, and how strong and beautiful of a person you are, for thinking of them and how much you loved them. It gives you peace of mind knowing that when you leave this life, your family will never question that you loved them for even a second. This is your last strongest statement to your family."*

Qualify Budget

There are three approaches to qualify a prospect's budget:

1. Presenting three options based on their final wishes

2. The top down method, where the agent starts high and goes down in price
3. Asking prospects what monthly amount they can afford to pay for their Final Expense plan

With the first approach, the agent will quote prospects three different amounts based on their final wishes: usually $3,000, $5,000, and $7,000 if they are getting cremated, or $7,000, $10,000, and $15,000 if they intend to have a traditional burial with funeral. Some agents write each amount on three separate cards, followed by the beneficiary's name, to get prospects emotionally committed to the solution.

Glen Shelton explains how he utilizes the three options approach to qualifying the budget:

> *"When it comes to discussing budget, I will present three options and explain that they can always come back for more. It does NO ONE any good if you select an option you CAN'T afford."*

The top down method is where the agent starts with an absurdly high monthly payment, like $200, and waits for the prospect to react to that. The absurd amount and the prospect's reaction to it can actually lighten the mood if agents handle the situation suavely. Most seniors will recoil and exclaim, "No way! I can't afford that much on a fixed income!" The agent might commiserate by saying, "I don't blame you, Mrs. Jones. That is a ridiculous bill to pay!"

Then the agent goes down from there, maybe to $150, and waits for the prospect to respond. The agent then goes lower and lower, feeling out the senior's financial comfort zone, until the prospect signals an amount that is affordable. This technique has the potential to help agents write larger cases because you aren't assuming how much (or how little) the prospect can afford.

Jason Eichmiller qualifies the health of the prospect and proceeds to qualify the budget with the top down method:

"And your age? Tell me about your health conditions and prescriptions over the past 5 years. (Then I "top down" sell...) The most coverage I can get you is x, and that is just y per month."

Most of the time they say they can't afford it, so we settle on a lower amount. One out of 10 times, they take it."

The only drawback with the top down method is the possibility of seniors overestimating their ability to pay the amount they choose. The average monthly premium for a Final Expense plan is around $50 a month. If the prospect chooses a monthly premium of $150, which is three times the average amount, agents could be setting themselves up for a first-year policy lapse. Of course, by building good rapport, delivering good customer service, and showing discernment for a prospect's affordability level, agents can minimize policy lapses — but still, you don't want to enable prospects to bite off more than they can chew.

When in doubt, if you sense that a prospect has chosen a monthly premium amount that may be unaffordable, just reconfirm that it is indeed an affordable amount. Some agents might recommend starting at a smaller face amount, and then the next year you can come back and ask how much more they'd like. This can reduce the initial shock to a senior's budget, while eventually giving them the coverage they seek, and helping the agent avoid a possible first-year policy lapse — so it's a win-win!

The third way to discern your prospects' budget is to simply ask what amount of money can they afford on a monthly basis for a plan that will pay for their final expenses so their family or beneficiary doesn't have to. This method is straightforward and sincere, and can close the lead by itself. Once you ask this question, stay silent. The first person who speaks loses, as they say in the sales world. Whatever the amount of money the prospect offers, as long as it's something, acts as a closing question and allows the agent to proceed to the application to qualify the lead's health.

Josh Doe explains how he qualifies the health before qualifying the budget:

> *"I ask the major things first: heart attack, stroke, cancer. Then I look at their meds. Then I pick a carrier I think may be a fit and have them read the health questions. As far as budget, I find an amount that is easily affordable on a monthly basis."*

Mike Shure qualifies health and then budget when presenting over the phone for Final Expense.

> *"In the past 2 to 5 years, have you had any heart, liver, lung, or cancer problems?"*
>
> *"Not everyone can afford a $10,000 Final Expense plan, but as parents we want to make sure we cover as much of the expense as we can afford. Now based on your budget, you might qualify for more than the price of your funeral, but it could also be less. Keeping your budget in mind, what can you allocate on a monthly basis?"*

Denise Rangel qualifies the budget and the ability of the prospect to qualify for less expensive Final Expense plans by asking about a checking account:

> *"When I am telling them about the guarantees, I tell them that there are discounts with some companies if you have a checking account to make your payment from, and ask them if they have a checking account. On payment, I ask them if I can find a plan for a certain amount, if that would fit into their budget without causing them any problems, and just work from there."*

QUALIFY HEALTH

After the agent qualifies a prospect's need and budget, and offers some education about the types of life insurance and coverage options available, the agent can then retrieve an application for the Final Expense plan he quoted. Of course, some agents prefer to qualify health first and then budget. A proactive agent asks about the prospect's health before presenting options, to avoid backtracking for new quotes as new conditions are revealed. In any case, by the time you pull out the application to officially qualify a lead's health, you should already be aware of any chronic conditions that may limit their coverage.

Using the application as the health qualifier in and of itself can be a closing technique. When coupled with the prospect's available budget and armed with the lead's "why's," agents can move confidently toward a sale, and proceed to health questions that indicate which level of coverage the prospect qualifies for.

Ron Wiza explains the benefits before qualifying the health and then the budget:

> *"This is called non-medical, non-physical type coverage. You don't have to be examined by a doctor to qualify. We do have to run through about 10 to 12 health questions that mainly have to do with major health issues, such as cancer or heart problems. Tell me, how's your health? Over the last few years, any issues like a heart attack, cancer, diabetes, or stroke? Any other health conditions I need to know about?"*

> *"As I'm going through the numbers and the actual cost, I'm going to ask you that you promise me that if what I am showing you is too expensive, that you just simply let me know. Okay? There are two ways we can look at the pricing: 1) You tell me how much you want to put toward your Final Expense planning each month and I can figure out exactly how much coverage that will get you. Or, 2) You can tell me how much you would like in coverage and I can figure out how much that investment would be per month. Which would you prefer?"*

After leads answer all of the health questions (usually between 10-15), you can let them know whether they qualify for immediate or graded coverage. Congratulate the prospect on qualifying for any level of coverage, and ask for a voided check and an ID to complete the application.

TYPICAL FINAL EXPENSE LIFE INSURANCE UNDERWRITING

Final Expense underwriting requirements can be less strenuous than underwriting for Medicare Supplements. Life insurance companies look at the chances of a person passing away (mortality). The chances of dying can be lower at certain ages than the chances of having a chronic condition (morbidity). Because life insurance companies want to minimize the number of gravely sick people they insure, they develop lists of conditions that usually cause a decline in coverage.

Conditions that can disqualify a lead from obtaining coverage include: being bedridden in a hospital, ALS (Lou Gehrig's disease), Down Syndrome, Cerebral Palsy, AIDS, amputations, cancer, dementia, or having been in a diabetic coma. Some companies may offer graded coverage for diseases such as: diabetes, cancer that ended four or more years ago, heart attack, hepatitis, illegal drug use, muscular dystrophy, and others.

Some companies might allow one chronic condition, but multiple conditions may disqualify a senior from coverage. This is where independent agents have an advantage, because they have access to various companies that may accept certain conditions or allow immediate coverage for particular conditions. By diversifying the number of companies you contract with and learning their underwriting requirements, you can reduce the amount of time it takes to figure out which company will accept a prospect's health conditions and prescriptions.

WANT A PIECE OF PHI?

With Final Expense sales, the agent usually has the option to complete the Phone History Interview (PHI) with the prospect or to rely on the insurance company to call the prospect and complete it later. There's no doubt that most agents hate dealing with the PHI; it's a hassle and can take a long time depending on the company, experience of the agent, and lucidity of the client.

However, smart agents realize that utilizing the PHI can increase persistency, because only interested and emotionally committed prospects will take time to complete the PHI, which solidifies their intention to obtain coverage. By taking the time to go through the PHI with a lead, agents reconfirm the lead's commitment to taking out a plan and increase the chances that the application process will be completed before the lead has time to succumb to buyer's remorse while waiting for the insurance company to call for the PHI.

Also, the PHI can act as a closing mechanism, making seniors verify their desire for coverage, some of their banking info (some), and their Social Security number. Doing this almost cements coverage in the eyes of both the agent and the prospect. There's no going back; they've taken care of the hassle of not having a plan anymore.

Final Expense Objections

Some leads won't have a reason why they asked for more information or requested a quote for life insurance. Some leads can't pinpoint an amount of money they're comfortable spending every month for a plan to take care of their final expenses. And some leads get all the way to the end of the application and, for some reason, throw up an objection or concern that could derail the whole process.

Agents must be ready for objections to pop up at any time, armed with the reasons why the prospect needs and wants a plan and equipped with the proper education that may put the prospect's concerns to rest. Here are some common objections you may get when you are presenting a Final Expense plan, specifically:

1. "I WOULD LIKE TO THINK ABOUT IT."

This objection can mean various things, perhaps:

A. The premium is too high and I'm not comfortable it would fit into my budget.

B. I don't trust the agent.

C. I can get a better deal somewhere else.

Any of those three possible objections could be the case. The agent's job is to question each possible real objection with prospects to root out the true reason why they want to think about it. In fact, you should consider yourself lucky to uncover Objection A because if the premium was too high and the prospect didn't speak up, it could've caused a lapse in the first year. A skillful agent would offer to lower the price and check back with the lead to see if the adjustment is more affordable.

If seniors think they can get a better plan or price elsewhere, they basically want to compare all of their options to make sure they are getting the best deal. Agents can handle these "shoppers" one of two ways. First, you could contract with as many Final Expense companies as possible, or at least illustrate all the companies via a quoting tool like Final Expense Quote Engine[8]. If you proactively show prospects price comparisons, provide education along the way, and genuinely show prospects you care about them, you could be building trust all along to help prevent this objection.

The second way to deal with the shopper's objection, if you are captive or if you failed to prevent this objection by comparing quotes, is by congratulating the lead on how they do business, noting that searching for a good deal is noble and respectable. Then, ask to set an appointment within one week to come back and take the application after they've had time to research rates. Don't rely on this lead for a sale, but instead focus on filling up your activity

[8] http://www.fexquotes.com/

with more leads and other appointments so that the occasional shopper who falls through the cracks isn't a big deal.

2. "I WOULD LIKE TO SPEAK TO ... FIRST."

Speaking to a family member can derail the whole process of putting a Final Expense plan in place. If the prospect has to talk it over with her kids, you'll often find the lead coming back saying something like, "My kids said they would pay for it," or, "They said, 'Don't waste your money, mom.'" Of course, most kids wouldn't hesitate to assure their parents that they'll cover mom or dad's final expenses. Unfortunately, that doesn't take the financial burden off of the kids' shoulders if there's not a plan in place.

There are two ways to deal with this objection, both before it comes up and after the presentation. You can preempt this objection by offering to present to the senior and anyone else involved in the financial decisions. Merely offering the option can assure many prospects of your intentions if you're willing to be held accountable to their family, caretakers, or fiduciaries.

The second way to deal with this objection is, if it comes up when you're attempting to close the lead and the prospect wants to consult someone else, you should ask two questions:

1. Whose responsibility is it to pay for your final expenses?
2. Would it be a burden for your loved ones to come up with $10,000 (or whatever death benefit amount) if you don't get a plan today?

The second question will motivate seniors who may be concerned about being independent, capable, and responsible about their financial decisions. If they feel it's their responsibility, offer to take their application again. If they feel they should still speak with their counsel, ask them the second question to make sure they are not stalling and putting off this vital task.

It can take more than 10 years to pay off $10,000 in credit card debt only making minimum monthly payments. Seniors who leave the burden of their final expenses to their loved ones could be indebting them for a decade or more after they pass away! This isn't the long-lasting type of legacy or memory most seniors want to leave behind.

If the lead answers these two questions, confirming their responsibility and agreeing that the burden would still remain (potentially for quite a long time), it could indicate a seriously interested lead. In that case, you should feel more comfortable that you might close the lead the following week. It's crucial to set an appointment before leaving to test the prospect's commitment to the solution. If the lead balks, this objection may stem from concerns centered around trust.

3. "I'M FINE WITH WHAT I HAVE."

You'll usually encounter this objection when initially calling the lead. If you hear this toward the end of the presentation when trying to replace or add on to what the senior already has, it can mean one of two things:

A. The premium difference/savings isn't enough to warrant a change.

B. The prospect has no need for more insurance.

The best way to overcome this objection is through a more thorough fact-finder. Beyond a funeral, burial, or cremation, many final expenses aren't even considered. It's the agent's job to ask prospects if the possibility of **medical bills, credit card debt** or other **loans,** the **loss of social security income for the surviving spouse,** or **probate expenses** could be cause enough to reexamine their current plan's death benefit amount.

4. "I CAN'T AFFORD THE PLAN."

This objection can either show up in the beginning or the end of the presentation. If you get this objection in the beginning, you should ask the lead who's responsible for covering their final expenses. If they affirm it's their own responsibility, you can then proceed to finding a more affordable price. Finding the absolute lowest price they are willing to commit to monthly, is paramount for these leads. Some agents won't bother to write a small $2,000 plan, but the smart ones might consider it because:

1. You never know if a senior might be able to afford additional coverage later on.
2. You might earn referrals from this client later on.
3. You could possibly try to cross-sell them a Medicare Supplement, saving them some money to pay for their Final Expense plan.

Frank Bahr responds to objections about price or affordability by saying:

> *"Most of my clients are on a fixed income, that is why we start small with something affordable. Your family would definitely appreciate whatever you can do. What is it you need to think about? Usually that means you are concerned about the cost, is that right?"*

If you encounter this objection and turn it around, you should still be cautious; a wise strategy would be to set aside this commission in case of a lapse, and just draw off of it as earned.

Now that we took a look at how some agents qualify the prospect's Need, Budget, and Health, along with how to deal with some objections, it is now time we take a look at how Medicare Supplement agents go about qualifying and presenting their type of insurance.

CHAPTER 6B: HOW TO CLOSE MEDICARE SUPPLEMENT LEADS BY QUALIFYING, PRESENTING & DEALING WITH OBJECTIONS

One reason selling Medicare Supplements is a little different than selling Final Expense plans is that the order of qualifying is different. Usually when agents are selling Medicare Supplements, they qualify the senior's health first — whereas agents selling Final Expense qualify the need first.

1. QUALIFY HEALTH

Qualifying a Medicare Supplement lead's **health** before qualifying the **need** (which is the lead's assumed desire to want to save on Medigap premiums) accomplishes two things.

First, it helps agents manage their time more efficiently; there's no need to compare quotes for seniors if their health won't allow them to pass the insurance company's underwriting requirements. The second reason to qualify a senior's health is a "takeaway" sales technique, which is rooted in the scarcity principle. Taking away the possibility of qualifying for savings on a Medicare Supplement might make prospects take more interest in seeing if they qualify for the savings in the form of a lower monthly premium and/or lower future rate increases.

Joseph Smith qualifies the health before proceeding to budget qualification:

> *"What alphabet letter plan they have, their rate, height, weight, whether they are a smoker or non-smoker, then I ask five basic medical questions (diabetes, COPD, heart issues, cancer, and any upcoming surgeries)."*

Tom Massey also qualifies the health before proceeding to budget qualification:

> *"I represent over 15 of the main Medicare Supplement companies and they all underwrite differently. I need to know what medications you take and what major health conditions you've been treated for in the past three years so I can see how much money I can save you for the exact coverage you have now."*

When selling Medicare Supplements, agents qualify a prospect's health early in the process by confirming the senior's ability to pass underwriting. This may be more challenging or complex, for the reasons we'll explain below.

Typical Medicare Supplement Underwriting

Medicare Supplements are tougher to qualify for than Final Expense plans because life insurance companies look at *mortality,* which is the chance of passing away at a certain age, while Medigap insurance companies look at *morbidity,* which is the chance of paying for services related to chronic health conditions.

Seniors may have comorbidities, or multiple chronic conditions like a combination of high blood pressure, high cholesterol, obesity, smoking, or diabetes. One of these conditions by itself wouldn't necessarily exclude a senior from coverage, but two or more might.

Major conditions like cancer, insulin-dependent diabetes, heart attack, stroke, being wheelchair bound, ALS, Multiple Sclerosis, or having an organ transplant within the last five years usually signal a decline for most companies. Being hospitalized twice or more in the past two years is another disqualifier. There are more conditions that are even rarer and harder to pronounce on the applications for coverage; agents should consult the most competitive companies in their area to see what other conditions may apply.

In addition to the conditions an application may screen for, be sure to consult the company's prescription decline list with any prescriptions the senior may be taking to rule out a decline.

GUARANTEED ISSUE (GI) VS. INITIAL OPEN ENROLLMENT (IOE) VS. ANNUAL ELECTION PERIOD (AEP)

There are three periods that are critical to seniors qualifying for Medicare Supplement plans (in order of importance):

1. Initial Open Enrollment (IOE)
2. Guaranteed Issue (GI)
3. Annual Enrollment Period (AEP)

Initial Open Enrollment is a six-month period that starts when seniors turn 65 and/or first get on Medicare Part B. During this period, seniors can get any Medicare Supplement plan from any company in their state, and the company cannot ask any health questions.

Seniors with more chronic health conditions should consider their choice of supplements, because once they get a supplement, there's no changing it due to underwriting restrictions. That's why it's important to go over the difference in premiums and rate increases between the plans and companies, so seniors understand any long-term implications.

Mark Barendt asks T65 leads:

> *"What is your biggest worry about Medicare? Do you have friends that have had big surprises because they didn't have this coverage? Are you worried about paying doctor's bills?"*

The **Guaranteed Issue** period happens when:

- A senior moves out of a Medicare Select or Medicare Advantage plan's service area.

- A senior is dis-enrolled from Medicaid.
- A senior leaves his or her previous employer's plan (or COBRA plan), whether voluntarily through retirement or because the employer discontinued its medical plan.

Only during these times can a senior get a Medigap Plan A, C, F, K, or L from any insurance company in the state. Although not all supplements are available for guaranteed issue, it's wise for agents to at least educate seniors on the differences between F and G to give them an option of lower monthly premiums and traditionally lower rate increases — plus the agent can earn full commission for enrolling a senior in Plan G, whereas commissions can be substantially reduced when enrolling a senior in a Medicare Supplement on a GI basis.

DUDE, WHERE'D MY COMMISSIONS GO?

An agent is typically paid little to nothing for guaranteed issue cases placed with companies. A company will either pay the agent a double digit commission and/or restrict renewals for a GI case. A smart agent will use this opportunity to still deliver meaningful service by helping the senior enroll, which might lead to possible cross-selling opportunities and referrals down the road.

The **Annual Enrollment Period** is a set time of year, October 15th through December 7th, when seniors can enroll in a Medicare Advantage plan or a Part D prescription plan (never both).

Many seniors confuse these three periods, so it's vital that agents educate their clients and prospects about what each period means for them. It's not uncommon for seniors to think that AEP is the only time they can change their supplements, when the opposite is true; they can only change supplements if they:

1. Can pass a company's underwriting requirements
2. Have a GI situation (see choice of plans above)
3. Enroll during IOE

SPECIAL STATES WITH ANNUAL EXCEPTIONS TO UNDERWRITING

The first type of annual exception to underwriting is found in two states: Oregon and California. These states' insurance departments have created rules allowing seniors the opportunity to shop their rates every year, in hopes that seniors save money and keep the insurance companies operating competitively.

The second type of annual exception to underwriting is Missouri's Medigap Anniversary Rule. On the annual anniversary of a senior's enrollment in a Medicare Supplement, the senior is allowed to shop the Medigap plan without having to pass underwriting.

2. EDUCATING AND INCREASING TRUST

After you qualify that the senior's **health** status will pass underwriting, and before putting together a comparison quote to qualify the **budget**, you should educate or reconfirm with the senior how Medicare Supplements function and address the implications of switching to the same plan with a different company, by explaining:

A. That all Medigap plans are standardized by federal law, which means they all have the same benefits from insurance company to insurance company; the only difference is the price the senior pays for a supplement.

B. How billing works when it comes to supplements. The doctor bills Medicare, then Medicare decides whether the bill is a covered expense, then Medicare sends the bill to the consumer's insurance company to pay whatever Medicare didn't pay. The supplement company cannot decide to cover Medicare approved expenses on a per-item basis. However, the supplement company can decide not to cover any expenses from a preexisting condition for the first six months if the senior didn't have creditable medical coverage up to 63 days before enrollment.

C. That there are no networks when using a supplement; seniors can go to any doctor that accepts Medicare as a form of payment. This also means they can go to any hospital in the country, as long as the hospital accepts patients who have Medicare.

Todd R. King cultivates trust and rapport by explaining how Medicare actually works, which distinguishes him from other agents who skip over this misunderstood subject:

> *"I simply educate the prospect on how their bills get paid by Medicare and the insurance company. Most will say they've never had that explained to them. That's where you really build trust explaining how billing and Medicare works."*

If you can educate seniors on these three aspects of Medicare Supplements, then you've completed the majority of education they'll need to start comparing other insurance companies' pricing for the same type of Medigap plan they currently have. Through this education process, the agent continues building trust and credibility to prevent various objections later on.

Ron Van Deusen compares the standardization of Med Supps with shopping for appliances, to simplify the concept:

> *"I like to use the metaphor of shopping for a television:*

"If two stores have the exact same TV and one is $400 cheaper than the other, which one will you buy? Then why not do the same smart shopping on your Medicare Supplement?"

Tom Massey educates Med Supp leads on the process of saving money on their Medigap plan insurance, just like auto and home – the senior has to re-shop it every two to three years.

"The benefits of a cheaper Medicare Supplement for a similar Plan F is the monthly savings. I ask prospects, "Why pay more for the exact same thing? Whether you're on a tight budget or just don't like overpaying for things, you might as well save money when possible." I explain that this is common practice with Medicare Supplements, to change about every three years. As the price of supplements go up, new ones with lower premiums come out."

MEDICARE EDUCATION: T65 VS. T67

There's a different amount of education needed with leads who are turning 65 and first entering Medicare, and possibly comparing the differences between a Medicare Supplement and a Medicare Advantage plan, as opposed to T67 leads who have been on a Medicare Supplement plan for some time and may be experiencing rate increases.

After going through the differences between Plan F and Plan G, **Bob Vineyard** asks prospects:

"Would you have a problem paying a carrier $300 per year to pay a $183 claim?"

Then after comparing Plan G to Plan N he asks prospects,

"Would you be willing to pay a $20 doc co-pay if you could save another $200+ per year?"

Of course, it depends whether the agent is AHIP certified and contracted to sell Medicare Advantage plans by any companies, if he'll be able to show the prospect actual plan comparisons. It's important to note that CMS forbids the use of telemarketing and cold calling to establish initial contact with Medicare Advantage and Part D prospects. If you get a referral from a telemarketed lead, like if the lead's spouse is aging into Medicare (turning 65), then you are allowed to present any Medicare Advantage plans you're qualified to sell, without fearing CMS penalties.

Agents can still illustrate general differences between a Medicare Supplement and a Medicare Advantage plan if they don't get into Medicare Advantage plan specifics. If the lead wants a Medicare Advantage plan, you can politely excuse yourself from helping that particular lead in order to stay compliant with CMS guidelines. An advanced agent may attempt to cross-sell the lead if he also sells Final Expense plans, but this may maximize the amount of effort needed to get the most out of his lead budget.

Plan F Vs. G Vs. N

Agents looking for maximum savings for a senior might recommend Plan G or N if the senior is on Plan F. In Chapter 1, we described why Plan G and N usually offer a substantial savings because of the decrease in monthly premiums and typically lower rate increases compared to Plan F.

To illustrate the differences in rate increases, it's important to convey to the senior that Plan G and N require the senior to pay the annual Part B deductible before the plan starts paying toward any health care expenses.

Also, companies offering Plan G and N are not required to take seniors who are eligible for a supplement under Guaranteed Issue rights. So a senior could only qualify for Plan G or N one of two ways:

1. During the Initial Open Enrollment of a senior turning 65 and going on Medicare for the first time.

2. Passing the health underwriting requirements of the company offering Plan G or N.

Because Plans G and N make seniors responsible for paying the annual Part B deductible, it lowers the amount of money these companies pay in claims compared to what Plan F must pay to cover the deductible for seniors. The fact that Plans G and N theoretically could have healthier people enrolled is the reason why Plan G or N may have lower rate increases compared to Plan F. Plan N may have more monthly premium savings and lower rate increases because seniors are responsible for any doctor and emergency room co-pays, in addition to the possibility of excess charges that a medical provider who doesn't accept Medicare assignment might bill above and beyond what Medicare covers.

Tools to Educate Seniors on How Medicare Supplements Work

Robin Penrod educates Med Supp leads using the CMS Medicare Manual:

> *"I ask if they have the 'Medicare & You' book, where I point out specific pages to discuss. If they have an email, I will email this to them. I use Wonder Bread as an example: Walmart may sell it for $1.50, but Kroger may sell the same loaf of Wonder Bread for $.99. Same bread, same packaging, same benefits, just a different price. It is a simple example, the senior crowd recognizes the name Wonder Bread, it is something they can relate to. Medicare Plan F allows you to see the same doctors, specialists, and hospitals just like Wonder Bread, just paying a better price, because I have shopped for you. No need to drive all over town to get the best price. I know which carriers have the lowest cost for the exact same item in their county."*

The easiest way to educate a lead on how Medicare works is by using the official U.S. government Medicare handbook, *Medicare &*

You,[9] or Medicare's *Guide to Choosing a Medigap Policy.*[10] Both are usually provided annually by CMS in electronic form at the http://www.medicare.gov/ website.

Justin Bilyj re-educates the prospect with how Medigap plans work:

> *"While I am researching rates to see if there's any possible savings for you, did you the get the 'Medicare & You Guidebook' when you signed up for Medicare? If you are like any of my clients you probably use it as a paperweight, but I coach everyone to read it every year as the new edition comes out, so they can keep up-to-date with any changes in Medicare."*
>
> *"If you turn to this year's edition, to page 92, you will see that it says right there that all Medicare Supplement companies are required by Federal Law to have the exact same plans with the same benefits, the only difference is the price you pay."*
>
> *"So in other words a Plan F with COMPANY or COMPANY is the same Plan F that COMPANY or COMPANY has, the only difference is the monthly price."*

Agents selling over the phone can ask prospects to follow along in the guidebook as you review the sections, or invite prospects to a web conference with screen share capabilities where you can open a copy of the guides on your computer while sharing your screen with them in real time. For the average Medicare Supplement agent who primarily sells over the phone, it's wise to preface these web-sharing opportunities by showing seniors:

1. A copy of your insurance license
2. Your contact info for future reference

---

[9] https://www.medicare.gov/pubs/pdf/10050.pdf
[10] https://www.medicare.gov/Pubs/pdf/02110-Medicare-Medigap.guide.pdf

3. Pictures of your clients and possible testimonials
4. Anything that displays you in a friendly, caring, and professional manner (like family photos)

Agents can also review:

- any previous videos they've made comparing Medigap plans with other plans
- any media mentions about them or their agency
- their own agency website
- possible awards for service

Loran Marmes expertly uses video in order to educate and build trust with leads:

> *"I prefer to email them a video on either Plan G or a basic one on how all Medicare Supplement companies must provide the same benefits. Getting the email is key, because I will 'touch' or contact them around their birthday after they get another rate increase."*

Chris Fonner tries to avoid turning off seniors by not asking them questions until he can get them on a screen share webinar in order to build instant trust and credibility, so that he gets more honest and accurate answers to his questions.

> *"I do not ask questions, I have them on a webinar and it automatically gets them involved."*

Even if the senior doesn't have email or the ability to use a computer, resourceful agents will mail the senior some or all of these materials, or just rely on the senior having a copy of either Medicare guide. This education process is a critical opportunity for agents to cultivate trust by creating an atmosphere where seniors feel that your main priority is helping them understand their options — not just trying to earn a commission.

Of course, it's important for the agent to distinguish between seniors who want more information in order to make a decision that will save them money on their supplement, versus those who are simply asking for you to mail them info to get you off their back. The first type of senior is legitimately interested; the second is just giving a typical objection response.

3. Qualify Budget with Quote Comparisons

Qualifying the lead's health and understanding of how Medicare and Medigap plans work will pave the way for the agent to start comparing and presenting different companies' rates for Plan F, G, or N.

It's up to the agent to decide whether to bring up Plan G or N. You'll know to bring up Plan G or N if:

- You think all seniors should know about all their Medigap options and this additional option would help them save more money than what a cheaper Plan F can afford, even after the deductible, etc.
- You think there's enough of a savings to switch the prospect to a cheaper Plan F, leaving the possibility of bringing up Plan G and N the following year after the lead gets the first rate increase.

Jeff Cornelius explains how he gets leads involved as he educates them about Medigap plans:

"First, I review the Medicare Supplement standardized plan chart. Usually, we have highlighted Plan F, G, and N. When looking at the differences with Plan F vs. Plan G, I have clients write down the annual cost of the Plan F Medicare Supplement, which in this example was $1,560. Then I have them write down the annual premium for a Plan G, which happens to be $1,200. I then ask them what the cost difference is, $360, so I point out that

Plan F is asking them to pay $360 more to save them from paying a $183 Part B deductible."

Joseph Smith finds it useful to get leads involved with calculating their possible savings:

"When it comes to comparing Plan F and Plan G, I have prospects write down their current plan and the cost of a Plan G with paying the deductible. Then I ask them to do the arithmetic and ask them to choose which plan they'd rather have."

Jeff Erb tells those who don't really use their plan:

"How does it make you feel to have that significant of a price increase (or pay that much every month) when you have not really used your plan at all?"

During the comparison of the Medigap plans, agents begin qualifying the senior's budget. This is not the same as a Final Expense agent qualifying a lead's budget, because the Medicare Supplement agent qualifies the lead's budget by:

1. Bringing up the fact that the senior may be on a fixed income.
2. Asking the senior about any previous rate increases.
3. Breaking down the act of enrollment into a shopping analogy.
4. Illustrating what the savings could amount to over time.
5. Finding out what they would do with the savings.

4. Qualify Need

The Medicare Supplement sales process is almost the reverse of the Final Expense sales process, because you're not trying to *sell* prospects an additional bill; you're trying to *save* them money on an existing bill.

The Medicare Supplement agent automatically assumes the senior has an inherent need to save money when living on a fixed income. You're not quantifying how much they can afford to pay every month (as with a Final Expense plan); you're qualifying how much the potential savings mean to them. Because of this, qualifying the budget and qualifying the need happen simultaneously when selling Medicare Supplements. The assumed need is confirmed when the agent compares plan options and prices for the senior.

Robin Penrod gauges a lead's assumed need of saving money by qualifying the savings in terms of what it allows the senior to accomplish with a freed up budget:

> *"With regards to their budget, I generally empathize that we are all on fixed incomes and a savings of $X amount a month provides extra income for other necessities or a trip to see the grandkids, etc. I also listen as we are talking and try to find a good reason why to change, and then loop it back to that hot spot when closing."*

Jason McKenzie references living on a fixed income in order to illustrate his unique way of comparing the monthly savings to receiving a raise in income:

> *"Mr. or Mrs. Jones, Social Security isn't going to give you a substantial raise; we know that. I'm offering you a $XX raise starting next month."*
>
> *Then I follow up with, "We can all use a little extra each month."*

Joseph Smith qualifies what the savings mean to the senior's budget:

> *I ask the prospect, "If we are able to find a savings of $30 - $75 per month that you are spending on your Medicare Supplement, would that amount of money help out each month?"*

Justin Bilyj quotes the prospect and then quantifies the savings by checking with the prospect to see what that amount means to them:

> *"And based on what you told me, Ms. Jones," referencing the health questions previously gone over, "and looking at all the companies in the state that have plans for your area, you should be paying (dollars) per month for:*
>
> ***Plan F:*** *"the exact same plan which has the exact same benefits, same doctors, and same hospitals."*
>
> ***Plan G:*** *"a Plan G, which as I said is almost identical to the Plan F, except the annual Part B deductible which is (dollars) per month this year. After the deductible has been satisfied, the Plan G acts like a Plan F for the rest of the year covering everything like your current plan does."*
>
> *"This is an annual savings of (dollars) per year for your family, which is about (dollars) in three years. What would you do with that extra money going back into your pocket every month?"*

Debbie Majher qualifies a lead's budget in terms of the possible savings available:

> *"What kinds of things could you do with that extra money in your pocket each month? Since you're on a fixed income, would an extra $XX a month help you meet your needs?"*

It's Not Always About Price, Dummy!

Of course, need isn't always based on price; it can be something else intangible to the senior. A good agent will ask the senior what they currently like about their plan, and what they dislike about it. This will enable the agent to address these potential hidden deal-breakers that might not be centered around price.

Philip Arko qualifies the lead on what they like and dislike about their current plan, to build those benefits back into the presentation when he presents another company's plan:

> *I ask, "What do you like most about your current supplement?" and then I ask, "What do you least like about your current supplement?"*
>
> *I also find out what letter plan they are in.*

Jeff Cornelius educates leads about standardization:

> *"I see that you have a Plan F. What do you like most about your plan? Mr. Smith, I am sure you are aware that, by law, all Medicare Supplement plans are the same and the only difference is premium, correct?"*
>
> *"So if we can find another Plan F with a lower rate than you are currently paying, which would allow you to have the same sense of protection, just at a lower rate, would that help you out?"*

If the senior:

1. Trusts the agent
2. Knows how changing Medicare Supplement plans works
3. Is happy with the savings
4. Is healthy enough to pass underwriting
5. Has any other important benefits also reflected with this choice

...then the agent can safely ask for the prospect's Medicare card for enrollment, and start filling out the application.

Jacob Anderson closes leads with the health takeaway close right after reminding them of the plight of other seniors living on a fixed income:

> *"Mr. Jones, Social Security didn't give a cost of living raise this year. Lowering your monthly premiums by $40, $50 or more can effectively give you more discretionary spending, which will help with your other expenses. Would this help you?"*
>
> *After they say "yes," he says:*
>
> *"Good. Let's take a few minutes and see what you qualify for."*

Justin Bilyj closes for the plan enrollment by assuring the prospect of the application process itself:

> *"Ms. Jones, the whole application process is easy and seamless. I do everything here on my end, I submit the application to the company, and they will call you within a day or two to confirm the health questions we just went over. After they call you to confirm the health questions, it generally takes about two to three days to find out if you have been accepted or declined."*
>
> *"It's important to note, Ms. Jones, no one's going to cancel your old policy until you have your new policy in hand and you see:*
>
> ***Plan F:*** *"that it's the exact same plan, same benefits just at a lower more affordable monthly amount."*
>
> ***Plan G:*** *"that the plan is a Plan G, which takes all your same doctors and hospitals, and that it is identical to your Plan F, except you must pay the one-time annual deductible, after that the plan acts like your Plan F for the rest of the year."*
>
> *"After you're assured that everything is the same, we can call up your old coverage to tell them you don't need them anymore so you aren't double billed."*

"All I need to get this started is for you to get your red, white, and blue card..."

Medicare Supplement Objections

As with Final Expense sales, Medicare Supplement agents will find objections throughout the sales cycle — in the beginning when you contact the lead, while presenting different plans, when quoting plan options, all the way until the closing when you ask for their enrollment. Whereas most Final Expense objections at the end of the presentation center around price (because you're selling them an additional bill), objections for Medicare Supplement sales center around trust and education.

Robin Penrod increases rapport and trust by not only answering a prospect's concerns or questions, but also relaying personal experience:

> *"I use phrases like: "I get that question all the time, glad you asked, most folks aren't aware of that." My goal is to make them feel that they are not alone in their fear, and their questions are normal. I tell them how I got into Medicare; my mother became very ill on Medicare and I had to learn how to navigate the system. Boy, was I surprised to learn we could purchase the same plan from different carriers for less money. Sitting in the hospital, I realized a lot of seniors don't have someone to help who really cares about their health, and I knew I had to help. This is my true story, so when I share this with them, they can hear it in my voice and that inspires a lot of trust."*

Here are some common objections you will hear during or after a Medicare Supplement presentation:

1. "I don't want to switch plans or companies."

Even though the savings may be great, sometimes more than $1,500 for the year, the senior may distrust the rates the agent quotes as "too good to be true." The only way to overcome this objection is to build a good professional rapport and make seniors see you as a concerned agent. Many agents selling Medicare Supplements, especially with telemarketed leads, aren't local to where the prospect lives. The best thing these agents can do is make themselves as personable as they can. Here's a list of ways to appear more personable and trustworthy when selling remotely to effectively educate the prospect on how Medicare Supplements work:

- Use screen-sharing technology to show seniors your webcam, your quoting software, a picture of your insurance license, and any pictures of family and clients.
- Send them something by mail that goes over what you have shown them.
- Send them an email with the same information.
- Send them a DVD or link to a video through an email that explains everything you went over with them.

Justin Bilyj responds to a prospect who hasn't heard of a particular company:

> *"You haven't heard of COMPANY? That's ok, they've been in business since (YEAR). They are a great company to deal with, they have great customer service, and I think if you give them a chance like many other of my clients have, you will find that they will be no different than your current company except your monthly payment will be lower."*
>
> *"I have your address as…"*

2. "I'M HAPPY WITH MY PLAN."

Most seniors are scared of change. Most would rather keep what they have, no matter how expensive it is, than risk losing it and:

A. Not have pre-existing conditions covered

B. Find out their doctors don't accept their new supplement

C. Not be admitted to their hospital in the case of an emergency

D. Be subject to low-ball rates with higher rate increases down the road

Jason McKenzie qualifies a lead's happiness with their current company by telling them what he did for his other clients:

"I understand that you're happy with the company but probably not with the last rate increase you got from them. I also write a lot of said company and like them as well, however, I have a lot of clients that are very unhappy about the last rate increase. So what I have done for them is found another A-rated company with the same Plan F/G and requalified them at a much lower rate."

Justin Bilyj reminds the prospect of the common sense approach to shopping for Medigap plans while proceeding back into the application:

"Ms. Jones, I am sure you agree that since these plans are identical in every way, there's no logical reason to spend more than you have to, right?"

"I mean if you are going down the street and you see gas for $1.50 on the right and you see gas for $2.50 on the left, you are going to go the gas station on the right, right?"

"I have your address as...."

Tom Massey reminds leads that future chronic conditions may impede their ability to change and save money later on (regardless of how unaffordable premiums may get in the future):

"How high will your Medicare Supplement premium have to get before you'll change? What will you do when you want to change, but your health won't allow you to qualify to make a change?"

If you establish trust and credibility by showing prospects your insurance license and testimonials from other happy clients, and if you effectively educate prospects about the standardization of Medicare Supplements and how Medicare billing works from any government Medicare guide, while showing them at the same time why you recommend the company and plan you are recommending, you can keep the objections to a minimum.

3. "MY PLAN PAYS EVERYTHING."

Medicare Supplement agents will hear this, or something to this effect, on the majority of their calls, due to the fact that more than 90% of seniors are enrolled in a Medigap Plan F, which pays **everything** when it comes to their medical care. Even if you don't mention another plan like G or N, and you're just changing the senior to the same Plan F but through a cheaper company, you'll still hear this objection.

When an agent hears this objection, the best way to answer their concern is by going over:

A. The Medigap plan chart to compare benefits

B. The Medicare & You Handbook[11]

C. Choosing a Medigap Policy[12]

For the objection, "I don't want to switch because it pays all the bills," **Joseph Smith** says:

> *"I am happy your plan pays your bills, because federal and state laws mandate that your Medicare supplement policy must pay the expenses it is required to pay. It pays well because it is supposed to pay, not because they are fond of you. As long as you stay with the same alphabet letter plan, it will pay exactly the same."*

---

[11] https://www.medicare.gov/pubs/pdf/10050.pdf

[12] https://www.medicare.gov/Pubs/pdf/02110-Medicare-Medigap.guide.pdf

Afterward, if seniors still have objections, then this isn't the real objection; it's a "smokescreen objection," masking their true concern, which is trust with the agent or the company. The best way to overcome this concern at this stage in the game is to have an online screen share to go over everything (if you haven't already), offer to mail them materials, send them to your website to watch one of your videos (if you have one), or to just offer them a couple of days to think it over. At this point, the best thing the agent can do is to give the senior some space, and not push too hard.

If you're unsuccessful with a follow-up call to close these types of leads, the next best thing is to ask if you can follow up with them later in the year to see how they're doing. Most seniors will consent to that in exchange for the opportunity to be "let off the hook" for now. The agent at this point has two options: bid these seniors goodbye until that time and put them in the pipeline to contact later, or try to cross-sell them on life insurance for their final expenses.

4. "I NEED TO TALK TO ... FIRST."

For the objection, "I need to talk to ..." **Joseph Smith** replies:

> *"I am glad you want to involve someone else with the decision. Do you feel it is important to ask your child/friend if you should save money? What do you think they will say if they knew you would save XXX per month for the same exact coverage?"*

As we've said before, proactive agents try to incorporate any possible objections into their presentation. This objection is best prevented by asking seniors if there's anyone they confide in before making plan changes. Usually it will be a spouse, child, nephew, or niece. If you want to bypass this objection without having to present twice, you can initially offer to show them the plan comparisons together, hopefully over a screen share (when selling over the phone) or in person (face-to-face selling).

Presenting to both the senior and their confidant can work in the agent's favor for two reasons. First, it prevents the agent from having to present twice, unless the other person has an odd or unpredictable schedule. The second reason is that it helps the agent close the lead if the confidant understands the rules of Medicare and the quotes comparison for the plans. This is an opportunity to not only create an ally by closing the lead with sound logic, but it could possibly earn the agent more business if the other person either wants to change plans/ companies or potentially refer someone else who does, now that you proved yourself the expert. If the agent offers to present to both people at once, and the senior doesn't want to go down that route, then this objection could also be a smokescreen objection that is again about trust. To overcome this, re-read the above recommendations on cultivating trust at this later point in the presentation sales cycle.

5. "CAN YOU MAIL ME SOME INFORMATION?"

This is probably the biggest smokescreen objection, even more so if you get this in person! The true objection is the same as what we've discussed already, just spoken with different words. The senior's concern comes down to trust, signaling that the agent did not sufficiently educate the senior or provide *all* of the information the prospect needs to make a decision.

Sometimes even after the agent goes through all of the Medicare publications, the senior's fear of change or loss of coverage can still prevent the agent from closing the lead. Whether there's any other information to give the senior or not, the agent really is at the mercy of the prospect. The best thing you can do is put them in the pipeline and drip on them over time, sending educational articles and cards to them to demonstrate your care and professionalism.

Justin Bilyj responds to seniors who would like to see things in writing:

"I can understand that; do you get email?"

Then I wait for them to open it and I tell them,

"I work differently than most agents, I do what is called "remote desktop sharing" which allows you to see ***everything*** *on my screen. After we go through my license and you see some testimonials we can take a look at all the companies side by side and you can see for yourself which company offers the best price for the exact same plan you have now."*

If I get this objection at the end of the presentation, I will only agree to send them info if I do what is referred to in the Sandler Sales system as an upfront contract or an agreement. I first try to ascertain whether the objection is a stall by being honest and upfront with the prospect,

"Mr. Jones, I appreciate that you want to see everything in black and white, but let me ask you, are you telling me this because you are just blowing smoke and not really interested?"

This forces them to either admit to me they aren't interested, or they start to ***sell me*** *on why they are interested.*

If they sell me good enough, I will mail out a packet, but only after we set another appointment to go over everything on the phone and that if they didn't have any questions, we would take an application to see if they qualified for the lower rate.

Maybe the prospect will come around and maybe they won't; the point is that you tried to go through all of the information available. If you have a polished online brand, educate seniors on all of the information, and put them into the pipeline for future follow-up or cross selling, you've done all you can to nurture the lead and extract as much value from each one as possible. Remember the old sales adage: "some will, some won't, so what." Just go to the next lead!

This brings us to the end of the Medicare Supplement presenting chapter where we learned the different ways agents qualify and quote the senior which leads them to collaboratively quantifying with the senior on what the proposed savings mean in relation to either a. the benefits staying the same, or b. having a nearly identical plan in exchange for a deductible (Plan G) or a deductible with co-pays and possible rare excess charges (Plan N). We also saw how to enroll seniors into a plan. Now the next step is to button up the sale and project some expectations for the client so that you can prevent any fears that they might have of being pushed into a plan and having the agent take off with his commissions. This is the beginning of what we call in the sales industry "customer service." Let's take a look at how we can start to serve our newly acquired clients as we go to the next chapter.

PART III.
AFTER THE SALE: KEEPING AND GROWING YOUR BUSINESS

CHAPTER 7: GREAT CUSTOMER SERVICE TO PREVENT LAPSES

YOU MADE A SALE! NOW WHAT?

Congratulations on completing the application process with a new client — but only half of the job is done at this point. The next several chapters talk about keeping and growing your client base over time through a combination of delivering great customer service to prevent lapses, cross-selling to maximize your services to each client, generating referrals, and staying motivated to keep pursuing new business while keeping existing clients happy. As soon as you take an application for Final Expense or Medicare Supplements, you start building the client's expectations about what will happen next. A good agent sets the expectation for the first three months right off the bat. After taking the application, explain that the insurance company's underwriting department will review the application and do a health background check (which may include the PHI if the agent hasn't completed it already). Let the client know how long it will take for underwriters to make a decision — usually anywhere from 3-5 days after all underwriting requirements have been met. Obviously, any missing pieces or additional questions along the way may lengthen the process before clients find out if they're accepted or declined.

Don't forget to leave behind or email any appropriate paperwork at the end of the sale, such as:

- Possible conditional receipt for life insurance
- Replacement forms
- Company brochure
- Plan benefits guide for Medicare Supplements

Garrett Ball finishes his appointments by telling the client:

> *"After you have your plan, I am an ongoing resource for you for as long as you have Medicare. You can call or email me any time, and I can answer any questions that you have related to Medicare."*
>
> *The main thing, though, besides what is said at the time of sale, is quarterly or at least bi-annual "touches."*

In addition to this paperwork, leave behind a business card or two. If you can afford to, spring for the ones with the magnetic backing. This card keeps your contact info handy, especially if it's displayed on a refrigerator rather than buried in a drawer (or the trash) among competitor cards. Remember, making your contact info handy and out in the open increases the chances of keeping your clients long term.

Todd R. King prevents lapses with a good button-up after completing the application:

> *"I take care of lapses right after the sale by letting them know that it's all about price (with Medigap plans). I let them know that I want to be their agent for the rest of their life and the only way for me to be that agent is I need to make sure they are with a company that isn't charging them too much, and we'll get them switched if the present company has too much of a rate increase. I let them know that I don't want them to have to pay one more nickel than they have to, as I'm sure they don't want to either!"*

Before you leave, be sure to thank clients for the opportunity to serve them, and reaffirm that you're there for them if they have any questions at all.

Policy Delivery

If agents have the option (meaning, if they work locally), they should personally deliver policies, so leads see and feel the customer service you deliver right after signing them up. It's a way for you to demonstrate to seniors that they made a good decision taking out the plan with you.

When you deliver the policy, walk the client through the plan, premium, and any other applicable benefits. A Final Expense agent will go through the policy, show the client what the premiums look like until age 100 or 121, at which time they don't have to pay any more premiums because the policy is fully endowed and contains cash value equal to the death benefit when the senior originally obtained the policy. Then go over the amount of the premium, confirming that the rate is guaranteed to stay the same if it's a Final Expense life insurance plan; if it's a Medicare Supplement policy affirm the first year's premium and let them know you will proactively shop their rates in the coming years in addition to keeping them abreast of what's going on with Medicare.

Also, take the senior through the guaranteed cash value schedule to show the build-up of cash value, reemphasizing that it's a permanent policy, because term policies that cancel before age 80 (sometimes later) may not be there when seniors need them, at a time when they might not be able to pass underwriting anymore due to possible chronic health conditions.

When Medicare Supplement agents deliver a policy, they explain whether the plan is the same plan that the senior currently has (Plan F), or a different plan like G or N. Either way, it's important to convey, like you did in the presentation, that their doctors and hospitals will take their supplement. If seniors switch to Plan G from Plan F, you'll want to cover the Part B deductible requirement and the possible benefits of switching, which include:

1. Lower monthly premiums (across most of the country)
2. Traditionally lower rate increases

3. Possibility of not having to pay the whole deductible if they only go to the doctor once a year for check-ups

If you're switching the senior to Plan N from Plan F or G, in addition to covering the Part B deductible as you would above, you should also mention:

- Doctor office co-pays no more than $20
- Emergency co-pay of $50
- Possible excess charges (though rare)

After going over any plan changes, verify the new premium and ask if the client has any questions. After answering any remaining questions, make it a point to tell clients that you'll call them in three months to check on them and see how they are doing with their new plan, because you like to stay close to your clients should they have any questions.

In addition to the three-month call-back, tell the client you'll contact them again on the policy anniversary. If you sold the client a Final Expense policy, the policy anniversary will be a perfect time to assess whether the client needs or wants additional coverage. If you sold the client a Medigap plan, the policy anniversary is when the rate will likely increase. You can mitigate the effects of the first rate increase for Medigap clients by reminding them that:

- All companies have rate increases; some more than once a year.
- The best thing they can do is switch to a more affordable company every year or two to keep rates low.
- They can choose plans that have historically lower rate increases.

CONSERVING YOUR LOSSES

It is easier to keep a client than to go out and get a new one, because all of the trust and most of the education has already been completed. Unfortunately, within sales and insurance specifically, agents must work diligently to conserve their business from lapses.

Lapses can hurt an agent's cash flow due to the charge-back created when the company asks the agent to return the advanced commission. Cash flow is the lifeblood of a lead program, and without it, the agent's book of business stops growing and the income starts to drop off.

Let's see how our collaborators handle lapses:

Lawrence Maloney says to clients who have lapsed a policy, after he gets them on the phone:

> *"Mr./Mrs. Smith, was the premium a bit too much? Well, I'm going to be back in the area tomorrow. We're going to create a plan that will be more affordable for you. Does 10 a.m. or 3 p.m. work best for you?"*

Jason Eichmiller explains how he handles Final Expense lapses:

> *"Lapses happen. I contact them, very persistently (because a dollar saved is a dollar earned) and figure out what went wrong: Did they lose their job or change bank accounts, or was it too much money? Then, I let them know that I care about them and their family, and that I'll do everything in my power to make sure they are affordably protected."*

Matt Mungia, MBA, talks about how he approaches lapses:

> *"I call ALL lapses to try and get back on the books. Sometimes it's as simple as the client has a new bank account and forgot to give you the new info. Sometimes you have to go rewrite them. But you must try to conserve business, especially starting out."*

Frank Bahr sympathizes with clients who lapse and asks questions to figure out what went wrong:

> *"What happened, did you change banks or get overwhelmed with expenses? Do we need to change the due date or decrease the monthly premium to get you covered?"*

Loran Marmes tries to use lapses as learning experiences:

> *"I don't do much to earn them back, I call and ask what more I could have done or if there is something I have done wrong. I make sure they have my number and tell them to call if I can ever be of help."*

Tamara Sasso explains how she saves lapses:

> *"I try to fix the (lapsed) policy right away, contact the client and try to save the policy in any way that I can. If it can't be saved, mark the clients to call them back later and try to help them, depending why they cancelled a policy or let it lapse. Sometimes clients don't realize it, and it just needs to be brought to their attention. Sometimes you need to write them a smaller death benefit to make their payments easier on their budget. If their budget has changed, find out why and how you can save it or change it. Never be afraid to call or show up on their doorstep."*

When it comes to selling Final Expense, agents want to maintain what's known as a "positive persistency rate" over the first 13 months. Ideally, the client will stay on the books forever, but because the agent is dealing with people who traditionally have a low annual income, the potential for lapsed policies is high — especially in the first year. Seniors may add and drop coverage once or more in their lifetime due to budgetary restrictions that tend to pop up.

A good agent will stay in contact with previous clients if he wants to be the first person they call years later, which can be a new commission if he writes the clients with a different company than before.

SERVICE FOR MEDIGAP RENEWALS VS. FINAL EXPENSE

Medicare Supplement agents can earn more than Final Expense agents if they can prevent lapses longer than the first year (hopefully indefinitely). If Med Supp agents can keep clients and switch them every two to three years to keep their rates low, they'll restart the six-year renewal commission schedule. Medicare Supplement agents can amass sizeable five-digit renewals every month by serving their clients and helping them save money, much like an auto or home insurance broker would, by regularly shopping their options. Accordingly, Medicare Supplement sales require consistent customer service every year to keep the client happy long-term.

Final Expense sales, on the other hand, require the majority of customer service efforts in the first year, trying to keep clients on the books to avoid a first year lapse. If Final Expense clients lapse their policies, it's likely because they can't afford it. A Medicare Supplement lapse is more likely because another agent lured the client away with a cheaper option. Of course, that may happen with Final Expense as well. **Both types of lapses may stem from affordability, so you may want to reevaluate your process for qualifying budget and comparing prices when initially selling the client.**

However, if you find that clients have decided to get a plan with another agent for either Final Expense or Medicare Supplements, you can do four things:

1. Offer to re-shop the market for them in hopes of keeping their business.
2. Remind them you have served them well and would appreciate the opportunity to review their plan to ensure they're making a prudent choice in regards to cost of

coverage (for Final Expense plans) or rate increases (for Medicare Supplement companies).

3. Let them go and try to learn from the experience.
4. File them into your pipeline system to come back to later and see if taking a plan out at that time makes more sense.

Jeff Cornelius explains how he calls back leads and what to do depending on why they left:

> *"Mary, I noticed that you have decided to replace your Medicare Supplement plan we put in place last year. I was calling to see if you had a problem with your previous plan."*
>
> *If they went with another carrier due to price, I ask if they mind letting me know which company and plan. If I think I can beat the prices, I will remind them that all plans are the same and provide them a quote with a lower plan, if available.*

Jeff Erb is persistent when approaching lapses:

> *"I ask them for an honest reason as to why they went with someone else, and then I ask for the opportunity to once again become their agent if there was nothing that I personally did that made them switch."*

Philip Arko will requote another company if required, but he will also let the client know about Medicare Supplement companies with unstable rate histories:

> *"I let them know that I can offer the same company if they want, and I re-quote them for the best rate. If the company they want to switch to has an unstable rate history, I will let them know that."*

Ron Wiza is quick to contact lapses:

> *"I will try to contact them immediately and see what the problem is. If I don't get ahold of them, then I will contact them again in 90 days and start a conversation with:*
>
> *"I'm calling to see if the timing is better now to reconsider that life insurance protection for your family?"*

Glen Shelton knows an agent must expect lapses if he's to be successful:

> *"If someone lapses during the first year for Final Expense, I will try to reach out to them via the phone and possibly email. If I can't get ahold of them after three attempts, I let it go. Lapses must be a part of your business plan or else you won't get anywhere."*

Todd Graves explains how he deals with lapses, selling Final Expense over the phone:

> *"If they have email, I put them on a drip email campaign that reinforces the benefits of having Final Expense insurance and shows cases of what happens to families when someone dies without being able to pay for final expenses."*

Of course, an agent can prevent all of this from happening in the first place by selling a competitively priced solution and simply contacting clients at least twice a year to stay top-of-mind. Another way to prevent clients from lapsing — whether it's because of budget constraints, forgetfulness, another agent selling them a plan, etc. — is by reminding them throughout the year of the reason they got a plan from you in the first place: either to protect their family from their final expenses if you sell life insurance, or to keep their health care expenses as low as possible if you sell Medicare Supplements.

Robin Penrod explains how to prevent lapses to begin with:

> *"I call 30 to 40 clients a week. A quick call: "Hi, how are you, everything going okay? Is there anything I can help you with?" It's usually a 3- to 5-minute phone call, or I leave a one-minute voicemail."*
>
> *"I answer my phone and return all phone calls the same day or next day first thing in the morning. I send a birthday card, a Thanksgiving card giving thanks to them as a client. I do a letter in September for open enrollment (with two business cards tucked in, asking them to pass those along to someone who may need to speak to an agent to see what their options are). I also do thank you cards to some folks that I didn't write. If we have a good connection and maybe they didn't qualify health-wise or they weren't ready right now or want to wait for AEP, I thank them for their time and let them know I am here should they have further questions; even though I am not their agent, I am here to help. Many times this leads to a referral to a friend, relative, etc."*

Whether it's a phone call, an email, a newsletter, or a card, the agent must solidify his relationship with his clients by maintaining spaced out "touches" or contacts over the year.

A Medicare Supplement agent needs to contact the client throughout the year more so than the Final Expense agent, especially past the client's first year. This is due to the changes in Medicare, like possible rate increases and changes to Social Security, etc. It's wise for the agent selling Medicare Supplements to contact clients before their policy anniversary and during AEP. Contacting clients during AEP also helps remind them that they don't have to requalify for their supplements at that time. If the agent is licensed and contracted to offer Part D plans, he can offer to shop and compare plans for the client to provide superior service.

Mike Smith explains the secrets to his success:

> *"I believe in multiple touches after the sale: a thank you card, follow-up card, birthday card. Selling is really just establishing rapport and trust from the beginning. But it certainly helps if you have very competitive carriers, as well. If you're typically within $5-$10, the policies won't be replaced. Even though lapses happen, ALWAYS CALL YOUR LAPSES! Sometimes it's just a simple fix, and you can get them back on the books."*

You can expect that Med Supp rate increases will happen around the client's anniversary because every year they get older, the supplement gets more expensive. Plan to contact clients a month to a month and a half before their policy anniversary to preempt the rate increases, before the change prompts them to seek an alternative solution. Some seniors, perplexed by the rate increase, may forget who their agent is or who they need to contact for more info. If you can reach out before the rate increase, it shows clients that you're attentive to their needs. You can re-explain how rate increases are inevitable, and that the only way to overcome them is by continually shopping rates around their policy anniversaries, like a home or auto insurance agent, and by also looking at plans that traditionally have lower rate increases, like Plan G or N.

Now that you have a process in place to deliver policies and stay in touch, let's look at cross-selling and asking for referrals. It's not mandatory to cross-sell or ask for referrals, but agents who maximize every dollar spent on their marketing plan tend to be the most successful.

CHAPTER 8: CROSS-SELLING

There are three main reasons to cross-sell or offer complementary types of insurance:

1. More commissions. If you've gone through all the trouble of marketing to, qualifying, and presenting to a client, why not use the bridge of trust you have built and see if they have additional problems that need remedying?
2. More persistency. It's a proven fact: the more policies an agent has within a household, the greater the agent's persistency, which guards against lapses.
3. More referrals. Clients that typically buy multiple policies from an agent trust the agent to a high degree, which makes obtaining referrals much easier.

Despite these alluring reasons, you should only approach cross-selling after you are proficient in the initial lead-in type of insurance you mainly prospect for.

Matt Mungia, MBA, has a wise warning to new agents:

> *"I tell ALL new agents to concentrate on one thing. Only after you have become good at that one thing do you need to offer anything else."*

How Should I Go About Cross-Selling?

An agent successfully cross-sells by either directly asking a prospect, or by passively marketing to the lead using email, newsletters, or cards in the mail. Asking the prospect directly is pretty easy and straightforward. There's no mystery to the process. A Final Expense agent might ask the prospect something like this:

Josh Doe is direct to the point:

"Who do you have your Medicare Supplement with?"

Looking at the above example I am sure you can easily guess how a Medicare Supplement agent would ask their client about their life insurance.

Or, if you prefer the passive method of slowly drip marketing leads with education and information about your other services, keep reading.

Robin Penrod waits until after the Med Supp client receives their policy before asking about final expenses, and also talks about Part D plans:

> *"I generally do a two-week follow-up call, making sure they received their card, remembered to show their doctor, etc. I will then ask about life insurance. I also do a letter four months after the sale and list what I do, and of course I call in September to get a jump start on a Part D prescription plan."*

When Should I Try to Cross-Sell Another Type of Insurance?

Some agents will attempt to cross-sell at various times in their interaction with a lead:

1. When the agent initially contacts the lead, and the lead isn't interested in the initial type of insurance offered.
2. If they present and don't sell a policy for some reason.
3. After they take an application.
4. After they deliver a policy.
5. Several months after they delivered the policy and they are following up on a fact-finder.
6. On the policy anniversary.
7. Various times through the year via drip marketing.

Glen Shelton cross-sells after completing a fact-finder:

> *"I do offer Medicare Supplements as well (and annuities), but on the initial appointment, I try to not get too involved in other products. It is more of a fact finding mission, and then at a later date, whether that's the policy delivery or a comprehensive review the following year, I know what product I can cross-sell."*

As you can see, there are many opportunities to cross-sell a lead or client. It is important not to overdo it and become known as a product-pusher; this can be a turn-off and possibly decrease chances of receiving referrals or even push the client toward a competing agent.

It's Easier to Cross-Sell Final Expense Than Med Supps

For a Final Expense agent, cross-selling Medicare Supplements can be a challenge. The majority of Final Expense clients are typically in lower income brackets (below $30,000 a year). Medicare Supplements have an average out-of-pocket premium per year of more than $2,000. The average Final Expense premium is around $50 a month, which is $600 a year. The Medicare Supplement can cost more than three times the amount of a Final Expense policy per year.

Due to the high cost of Medigap plans, there's a higher possibility of the Final Expense agent cross-selling Medicare Advantage plans instead.

A Final Expense agent willing to cross-sell Medicare Advantage plans might be able to maximize cross-sales through direct mail by sending clients a "Changes to Medicare" mailer. Not only is there a larger return on direct mail for Medicare than Final Expense — two to three times larger — but the extra return allows agents to:

1. Build up their AEP contact list.

2. Cross-sell Final Expense to the lead 48 hours afterwards, if they get a Scope of Appointment form filled out at the appointment (this is if there was a discussion of Medicare Advantage plans).
3. Possibly sell Medicare Supplements.
4. Cross-sell Part D prescription plans or build a list of leads to contact during AEP.

CAUTION

NOTE: It is forbidden by CMS to cross-sell a MA or PDP to telemarketed leads if they aren't already your clients. Please consult CMS marketing guidelines for further information.

Matt Mungia, MBA, is a fan of cross-selling MA plans to his Final Expense clients:

> *"I now offer Medicare Advantage. When I am leaving the house, I give them another business card and let them know about all the other things that I offer. Sometimes that leads to further conversation and further sales."*

It's important to note that when cross-selling Medicare Advantage plans (MA) or Part D prescription plans (PDP), the CMS marketing guidelines and rules for Medicare products could change year-to-year. It's up to agents to do their research every year to ascertain what is permitted. Due to the tenuous nature of MA and PDP marketing regulations, we leave it up to agents to pursue cross-selling those plans at their own risk.

Let's take a look how some other collaborators cross-sell their prospects and clients:

Jacob Anderson explains how he cross-sells his Med Supp clients Final Expense plans:

> *"I ask them if they need a plan for burial expenses, and help them use part of the savings towards the Final Expense. It helps that no new money is being spent."*
>
> *"With the money you save on your Medicare Supplement, you can take out additional life insurance so you'll have enough for your final expenses."*

Tom Massey takes the informative approach when cross-selling Final Expense to his Med Supp clients:

> *"I try to cross-sell all my Medicare Supplement clients. I ask them if they're set for life insurance. I tell them more than 40% of Americans have no life insurance and many who have it haven't upgraded it to keep up with inflation."*

Jacob Anderson cross-sells Final Expense plans to leads he meets with who don't necessarily qualify for a supplement but still qualify for life insurance:

> *"I tell them, because this company's rate is very low, they have to qualify for it medically. I tell them this only has to be done one time. I then ask them if they've been treated for any of the following in the last five years: heart attack, diabetes, cancer, or stroke. I then get all their meds, etc. Once I determine the carrier, I'll quote them. I proceed to ask all of the health questions on that carrier's app. Once I finish the sale or determine I can't help them because of health (or because they are on an MA plan), I ask if they have a Final Expense plan in place to cover the funeral cost. Just asking this question has led me to write two or three Final Expense apps a month on the side."*

For Medicare Supplement agents, cross-selling Final Expense can be somewhat easier than the reverse situation because they can propose taking a portion of the client's Medigap savings to put toward a Final Expense plan. This method, called the Frank Stastny method,[13] is utilized *after* the agent has saved the client some money on their Medigap plan, which allows the agent to demonstrate value first. Plus, it allows the client to purchase a Final Expense plan without additional money out-of-pocket, as opposed to buying a Final Expense plan without first freeing up the savings to spend.

Now that we've looked at the three reasons to cross-sell, when to cross-sell your leads or clients, and what to say, let's take a look at how to ask for or earn referrals.

---

[13] http://medicaretraining101.com/frank-stastny-training/

CHAPTER 9: GENERATING REFERRALS

Why You Want to Gather Referrals

Referrals, which are essential to an agent's long-term success, come from six possible sources:

- Prospects
- Clients
- Family members
- Friends
- Work associates
- Centers of influence like attorneys, insurance agents, accountants, etc.

There are various reasons why an agent would want to cultivate referrals; perhaps because:

1. Referrals are free.
2. There is an element of trust already established, making referrals easier to present to.
3. Referrals help build and endorse the agent's brand reputation.

Many seniors who have a need for life insurance or Medigap plans will ask a person close to them how they should go about finding a new plan or better rate for their current plan. The number and frequency of referrals will increase when agents:

- Position themselves as referable experts.
- Provide consistently great customer service year-in and year-out.

- Demonstrate value by shopping multiple companies.

EARNED OR SOLICITED?

There are two ways of obtaining referrals: earning them (passively) and soliciting them (actively). Some agents feel they should get referrals as a natural result of performing great customer service.

Tom Massey prefers to rely on providing good service to earn referrals:

> *"The best way to get referrals is to provide great service. I return calls the same day and get my clients' problems taken care of ASAP. When they buy, I let them know that I'll be glad to help their friends and family. I also send a thank you card after the sale."*

Josh Doe's success revolves around good customer service:

> *"I just try to provide good service and the referrals come naturally. I don't generally ask for them."*

Then there are agents who feel that actively soliciting referrals from prospects can improve an agent's bottom line. You may not always be able to rely on business flowing to you passively, so developing a program to directly solicit referrals can be strategic business development.

Frank Bahr actively asks for referrals after helping prospects find a plan:

> *"I hope I have been helpful to you and your family. Other than your immediate family, who are three friends you know would attend your funeral? Would it be okay to tell them about the service I was able to provide for you?"*

Final Expense Referrals Vs. Medicare Supplement Referrals

Medicare Supplement agents are more likely to receive passive referrals than a Final Expense agent, because Medicare Supplement agents typically provide more consistent customer service. There is relatively little servicing work needed after selling a Final Expense plan, but Med Supp agents stay in touch with clients regularly to discuss changes to Medicare, annual changes to Part D and Medicare Advantage plans, and rate increases — which keeps them top-of-mind throughout the year and gives clients more examples of their referable service.

Plus, seniors are far more likely talk with each other about their medical insurance, various prescriptions, and what they pay for them than they are to chat over coffee about final expenses, life insurance, and other morbid subjects.

Because Final Expense agents generally earn fewer referrals than Medicare agents, they might want to consider soliciting referrals more proactively to lower (and maximize) their lead budget. Here are some ways Final Expense agents can ask for referrals:

Todd Graves takes good notes and refers back to family members who might need coverage:

> *"After a policy is placed, I usually have a good idea as to family members like children and grandchildren, and talk about the unexpected death of younger loved ones, saying the time to cover them is when costs are low at a younger age. Then I go from there."*

Learn How to Ask for Referrals

It's not enough for an agent to simply ask for referrals. If you're going to ask for referrals, be strategic and specific with it. Asking blanket "who do you know?" questions without a qualifier will just confuse the senior.

Todd R. King has sage advice for new agents learning to ask for referrals:

> *"One of the first mistakes I see agents making when asking for referrals is to ask a blanket statement like, 'Do you know of anyone else who could use my help?' You have just given them the whole world to think about, and therefore most can't think of anyone. If you find out things that they like to do through your warm-up and presentation, then that will help you in narrowing it down. For instance, if they are a golfer or avid church-goer, you would ask something like, 'Do you know anyone you golf with that could use my help?' or 'Do you know anyone in your Sunday School class that I may be able to help?' It just helps them think about it easier. Be sure to leave extra cards, too!"*

Another popular option for agents to obtain referrals and increase the number of "touches" throughout the year is by using a passive but personal marketing service like SendOutCards. SendOutCards is a website where you can set up campaigns with pre-designed, personalized postcards or holiday greeting cards that you can schedule to be sent to your clients. This service is a very inexpensive set-it-and-forget-it marketing machine that allows agents to:

1. Stay in contact with clients throughout the year, which reduces the chances of them going to a competitor.
2. Remind pipeline leads of possible savings of switching plans if they haven't become clients yet.
3. Demonstrate thoughtfulness and genuine care for clients, which helps build relationships and rapport.
4. Obtain referrals.
5. Cross-sell other services.

Lawrence Malone asks for referrals by focusing on how clients feel after taking care of their final expenses:

> *"Mr./Mrs. Jones, how does it feel to have finally taken care of this? Alright, well if you don't mind, could you write down about five people who would also benefit from the peace of mind you have right now?"*

Brandon Webster trains his staff how to collect referrals after a sale this way:

> *"I have my assistant contact all clients after the policy has been received and issued. We always ask if they can give us 3-5 names of people they know who they want to make sure are protected just like them."*

Jeff Cornelius explains his passive referral strategy:

> *"I usually do not ask for referrals. I have a call/mail drip program that starts with a thank you card (with two or three business cards to share with friends) as soon as I send in the application, and a "what to expect next" email. Then I answer any questions via phone about two weeks out, send a summer postcard to stay in touch (around July 4th), birthday card with business cards, AEP letter or postcard, Christmas card with business cards, Happy New Year card that says thanks for your business, along with business cards and a calendar for the fridge."*

Tamara Sasso has a novel method of asking for referrals:

> *"I ask my clients if they know anyone else I can help, such as friends or family. I also get a page of contacts who would need to be called if they passed away, and call those contacts as well, with their permission."*

Debbie Majher explains how she cultivates referrals on top of referrals:

> *"We use SendOutCards and send small gift cards to reward clients for referrals."*

Justin Bilyj cultivates referrals with SendOutCards:

> *"I am a big fan of the book, 'The E-Myth Revisited,' which describes the automatization of the business processes similarly to Tim Ferriss' book, 'The 4-Hour Workweek.'"*
>
> *"Being able to send a card right after the application is taken, then another after they are a client, another cross-selling card for Final Expense three months later, and a renewal card one month before the anniversary helps me keep my clients happy, and I don't have to do anything but load the name and address into the site."*

Of course, you don't have to use SendOutCards; you can go to Vistaprint and design a similar series of cards. You can even sit down and handwrite a few cards or letters for special clients, though this method will be the least scalable as your client base grows. The set-it-and-forget-it automation (and/or the help of an assistant) is key to keeping your referral program running smoothly in the background of your business.

WHEN SHOULD I ASK FOR REFERRALS?

Agents have many opportunities to ask for referrals. Some agents will ask for referrals when they:

1. Make the sale
2. Deliver the policy
3. Months after enrolling a client
4. A year later after they have demonstrated good customer service
5. Systematically throughout the year
6. Or even if the prospect doesn't buy.

Glen Shelton asks for referrals, even from prospects who can't take out a policy due to health, timing, or affordability issues:

> *"I ask for referrals every time before I leave a house. Something I have found to work in my favor is if I sit down with prospects and the policy I offered just was not a fit for them, but I have already taken the time to introduce myself and what I do, I make sure to push for the referral at the end of the conversation. I noticed that some folks still would want to help me out even though they weren't ready to become a client at that time. They sometimes would happily refer me to a friend or family member."*

Possible examples of different types of cards are available on our website, along with additional information on how to set up a SendOutCards account to create a passive marketing machine. Now that you have a good idea on how to earn and ask for referrals, let's figure out what keeps agents motivated and on track. Selling a policy is one thing; it's another thing to be consistently selling policies throughout the year, building a pipeline lead list, and creating a passive marketing strategy to keep bringing in business.

CHAPTER 10: STAYING ON TRACK AND MOTIVATED TO KEEP SELLING & SERVING

To be a successful insurance agent, you have to efficiently juggle many different client interactions with a multitude of seniors in many different situations, who may be at different points of the sales cycle. Staying on track with your existing business while staying motivated to keep generating new business is a tricky balancing act that you'll always be adjusting as you advance in your career.

Agents have their choice of technologies to help them stay on track, through a combination of customer relationship management (CRM) tools and productivity apps. Both toolsets are necessary to minimize distractions, keep records up-to-date, and track "lead dispositions" (or details about where each client is in the sales cycle).

Also be sure to stop back periodically to the Lead Heroes website where more tools, tips, and strategies will be shared in upcoming posts!

CUSTOMER RELATIONSHIP MANAGEMENT (CRM)

CRM software allows agents to track various information about their leads, like:

- Plan and premium details
- Appointment schedules and reschedules
- Health conditions
- Beneficiaries or other family member info
- Contact details

- Other notes like hobbies, etc.

A CRM is one of the top tools an agent can utilize to stay on track by efficiently managing lead interactions and info. RadiusBob, Salesforce, and Pipedrive are some examples of CRMs that are popular with other insurance agents. Obviously, we don't recommend a new agent starting out paying for a sophisticated CRM because there are many free ones you can try out first. It's important to track what's going on with your prospects and clients so that you can maximize every dollar spent prospecting. Think of your investment in a CRM as a way to support and enhance your lead generation efforts.

Jason McKenzie explains how he uses a CRM to track his leads:

> *"I always follow up on old leads. The lead stays in my CRM and is called each time I am visiting some other lead in the area. Most of the time they have had another rate increase. Just because they don't want to talk one week doesn't mean their needs won't change."*

Productivity Apps

Technology can both help and hinder an agent trying to maximize his time. Let's face it: When you're stuck at your desk dialing leads, sites like YouTube can be a tempting distraction from your to-do list. But with the right productivity apps, you can use technology to your advantage to help you organize your day so you can contact more leads, or to help you overcome distractions and time-wasters.

The number one free productivity app that can help agents stay on track is the internet browser add-on, LeechBlock.[14] LeechBlock helps ward off distractions by blocking certain websites that you flag, according to the times that you choose. It's far too easy to find yourself checking your email or your Facebook feed, and wind up

---

[14] http://www.proginosko.com/leechblock/

on a tangent reading politics or watching funny videos. LeechBlock lets agents designate certain time-waster websites to block during their most productive times of day, which is typically 10 a.m. to 5 p.m.

WHAT INSPIRES AND MOTIVATES OTHER AGENTS?

Staying on track is half physical and half mental. You can have all the helpful technology in the world, but if you don't have a *reason* to be successful or a *motivation* to prospect and close leads, then you may not be pushing yourself to grow or giving your marketing plan a chance to succeed. Just as the client's "why" is critical to make your solution feel relevant to them, identifying your own "why" is critical to making your career feel meaningful.

In the book, "Secrets of Question-Based Selling,"[15] sales trainer/author Thomas Freese talks about two forces that either push or inspire salespeople to be successful: Gold Medals and German Shepherds.

Gold Medals are the possibility of positive experiences that will happen if you successfully close leads and make sales. Some agents are inspired by:

- Earning enough commission to pay off their house earlier than scheduled.
- Putting more money away for retirement.
- Taking their wives on lavish vacations or out to fancy restaurants.
- Splurging on a new fishing boat or set of golf clubs (or buying the wife some nice jewelry).
- Earning a trip based on sales production.

---

[15] http://qbsresearch.com/qbs-products/secrets-of-question-based-selling/

While some agents are motivated to run toward a Gold Medal, others are motivated to run away from a German Shepherd, or the possibility of negative experiences that agents want to avoid. Some of these negative experiences could be:

- Falling behind on their mortgage.
- Failing to keep food on their family's table.
- Not being able to go out and have fun.
- Failing as an insurance agent.

It's not uncommon for an agent to be pushed forward by both "the carrot and the stick."

It's not an either-or situation; some agents may have a large German Shepherd motivating them to keep food on their family's table, while simultaneously being inspired to help out others out as a reward in itself.

Here are some of the common Gold Medals and German Shepherds of our collaborators:

Joseph Smith recounts his desire for a career with a potential pay-off:

> *"What motivated me was earning a living and the long-term value of residual income."*

Jeff Erb has an easy way to track his success — his bottom line:

> *"Looking at my checkbook balance and not being satisfied with the number."*

Jason McKenzie talks about how a good lead source can make a difference in motivation:

"Having good leads makes it easy to pick up the phone when you know mostly everyone you call will at least hear what you have to say."

Frank Bahr sums up his goals pretty easily:

"My desire is to retire before I die."

Todd R. King explains how momentum drives him to keep prospecting:

"To me, (cold calling) was the hardest part of the job! I hated picking up that phone. But each and every time, once I started, it was a piece of cake to keep going. I just tried to remember what it felt like after the first call. The motivation was always the money to begin with, but most times, after talking with a prospect, it became a matter of helping them. Ultimately, helping them and being the hero was my biggest motivation."

Jason Eichmiller's family is his main motivation:

"I have a wife, three kids, and multiple homes. My wife doesn't work. Every day I think about how blessed I am to have this life, and I do whatever it takes not to screw it up. That means setting appointments, closing deals and getting referrals, constantly."

Justin Bilyj is motivated by creating and running a business entity:

"I love to not only help others with their insurance concerns, but what I love most about the insurance business is the ability to create an autonomous business machine that can make money for you with residuals."

Mike Shure is motivated by competition to out-sell his partner:

"Money. I want to make money and out-sell my business partner. Competition is a big motivator and part of my success."

Matt Mungia, MBA, loves to travel with his family, so that's his Gold Medal:

> *"Carrier trips! Travel is my family's favorite thing to do. That's enough incentive to keep me going."*

Ron Wiza is inspired by more humanitarian ideals that stem from helping seniors:

> *"Success breeds more success. I know if I get one, then I'll hopefully get another one. I enjoy not only the financial gain but helping these people when they don't know where to turn for help. There's a lot of satisfaction in that."*

If you want long-term success selling Final Expense life insurance or Medicare Supplements, you need to discover what motivates or inspires you more than anything to keep prospecting and presenting on a continual basis every day. Just like Tony Robbins talks about creating lasting change, agents need to know what acts as their fulcrum or "leverage" that will bring about the desired change or ideal behavior.

Organizing Your Schedule

Many agents fail to develop a rhythm because they don't maintain a schedule that allows them to focus on the task at hand. The worst thing an agent can do is start ordering leads without a time management plan in place. Having one will help you maximize your time and extract the most out of your leads. Here are some examples of how agents maximize their schedules to be more successful:

Todd R. King recounts his field schedule for the week:

> *"Mondays are for calling my leads and setting up appointments for the week. I start calling at 9 a.m. until 11 a.m., then start again around 3 p.m. to 4 p.m. and continue until 5 or 6 p.m. I try to set them on Tuesday, Wednesday, and Thursday. Friday is*

application processing day and usually a half-day. I rarely work weekends."

Nathan Robinson talks about his schedule for face-to-face sales:

> *"From the hours of about 9 a.m. to 3 p.m., I'm traveling on the road to visit with clients whom I have scheduled appointments with. These are clients who do not want to apply over the internet, and these are clients who do not like to be explained insurance over the phone."*

Ron Wiza describes his daily schedule:

> *"I am an early riser. I do paperwork at 6 in the morning. I do not call anyone till 9 a.m. I try calling the same leads at 9 a.m., 1 p.m., and 5 p.m. I have begun door-knocking and enjoy that much more and have better success. I see more people that way. Some people never will answer their phone if they don't recognize the number. If I have no success getting ahold of the lead, I turn it over to my appointment-setter for help. They are more patient than me when it comes to using the phone."*

Jason McKenzie describes his field schedule for the week,

> *"I call leads Monday and Tuesday and set appointments for Wednesday. Monday, I call mornings, afternoons, and evenings. Tuesday, same as Monday. Wednesday is my long day; I leave the house around 5:30 a.m. and run appointments till 7:30 p.m. On Thursdays, I turn in business."*

Jeff Erb is either dialing or presenting:

> *"I run any appointments in the morning that have been preset. During lunch time, I dial the phone; I also run any afternoon appointments that are set. After dinner from 7 p.m. to 9 p.m., I dial and set appointments for later in the week."*

Ron Wiza talks about mailing, calling, and when not to call:

> *"When I don't have any appointments, I'm at home calling prospects. I usually start calling these people between the hours of 9 a.m. to 3 p.m. There are some clients who do not like to be called before 10 a.m. I look at the client's age, and if they are over 70, I will not call them before 10 a.m. Clients over the age of 70 tend to sleep later in the morning. I almost never call clients in the evening unless they ask me to, or unless I cannot get in touch with them during the day. I also mail out letters to clients that I cannot get in touch with."*

Justin Bilyj presents how he goes about organizing his prospecting days:

> *"I get up around 6 a.m., get the news out of the way and prepare my day. I will call prospects or seniors no earlier than 10 a.m. I will make calls until noonish, then I will pick up calling again after 2 and go until 6-8 depending on if I am calling more Western states."*
>
> *"I try to group my appointments together towards the end of a calling block and work backwards."*

No matter how you decide to organize the day or week, stick to it. Group your tasks into time blocks i.e. call in blocks of time, do appointments in blocks of time, do paperwork in blocks of time. Wayne Cotton, proprietor of his own referral-based prospecting system, put together a free website for financial professionals wishing to stay on track called No Brown Days.[16] On the site he has an annual calendar to help agents plan their blocks of time out and organize their weeks. It's just too hard to pick up one type of activity, drop it real quick for another. Agents wishing to utilize

[16] http://nobrowndays.com/

nature's law of inertia will seize upon their momentum when grouping like tasks.

HIRING AN ASSISTANT

Our final suggestion for staying on track is to hire an assistant. Brought into the modern business lexicon by Tim Ferriss and his book, "The 4-Hour Workweek," a personal assistant or VA (Virtual Assistant) can help agents stay on track five possible ways:

1. Calling new and pipeline leads to set appointments.
2. Rescheduling no-shows.
3. Taking service calls.
4. Reminding Final Expense clients of their overdue premium, which helps conserve lapses.
5. Pre-screening leads to see if they have a need and qualify for a plan.

Frank Bahr is able to streamline his business with the help of an assistant:

> *"I prefer to work three long days, with as many appointments as possible, using an appointment-setter. Mondays are clean-up days with application and company requirements. Fridays are sometimes for training or I take the day off."*

Ron Wiza will contact his leads initially while his appointment-setter focuses on older pipeline leads:

> *"(I try) three times, then turn it over to my appointment-setter to keep trying. I say the exact same thing that I say to a new lead. Because these people can be hyper-responsive, they probably respond to same things many times a year and probably don't remember when they responded."*
>
> *"I treat unresponsive leads like a new lead when I reach them."*

One problem with assistants is that they will never be as aggressive with prospecting leads because the money used to pay for leads wasn't their own, so theoretically there's less concern to convert each lead into a client. However, if you can tie measurable outcomes to your assistant's performance and reward your assistant accordingly, it can inspire or motivate your assistant to do a more thorough job. One way to do this is to pay assistants a commission or "spiff" per application taken, number of clients obtained in a quarter, or per policy they prevent from lapsing.

It's up to the agent to determine the compensation structure. Where and how you find your assistant may dictate the average cost of that assistant's continued employment. If you found a virtual assistant on a site like Upwork, you may pay less than if you were to hire someone locally through job listings on Craigslist or in the newspaper.

Hiring an employee has various tax consequences, in addition to other considerations. It's wise to seek the counsel of a qualified tax professional before deciding to hire an employee. One way to avoid the messy consequences of taxes is to contract your assistant as an independent contractor rather than hiring one as an employee. This requires the assistant to be responsible for his or her own tax obligations, and you can simply deduct the cost of services as a business expense. Ultimately, heed our prior warning about consulting qualified legal or accounting professionals to assist with your employment questions.

When creating your assistant's phone script for qualifying leads, you'll want to add some verbiage to indicate they're calling from your office to see if seniors qualify for:

A. Medigap plan with cheaper rates but the same benefits, or

B. Final Expense plan to pay for their final expenses so their family doesn't have to.

It's up to the agent to decide how thoroughly the assistant should qualify a lead before setting the appointment. If you only want to deal with leads that can pass underwriting, you may want your assistant to ask general health questions before passing a prospect to you.

After the assistant verifies the necessary information, he or she can give prospects a choice of two time slots to decide which time best fits their schedule. If the agent/agency has any videos or brochures, the assistant can send these materials before the appointment to prep the lead on the agent's process and to show how professional and prepared the agent is.

APPOINTMENT SETTING SCRIPT

"Hello, is Ms. Jones/Mr. Jones there?"

"Hi ma'am/sir, this is Assistant with COMPANY, I am calling you concerning,"

DIRECT MAIL: *"the postcard you mailed back to us recently/a while ago regarding..."*

TELEMARKETED LEADS: *"the phone call from our office yesterday/last week regarding..."*

FINAL EXPENSE: *"the information on the state approved burial program."*

MEDICARE SUPPLEMENT: *"your Medicare Supplement, and whether you qualify for a lower rate for the same exact benefits you have currently."*

"It says here that your age is NUMBER, is that correct? Have you been hospitalized for anything in the last five years or experienced a heart attack, cancer or stroke?"

"Lastly do you smoke?"

"Alright, it takes about 15 minutes for Agent to go over everything and let you know what you qualify for. Our Agent is scheduled to be in your area/available for a quick meeting, let's see we have a TIME and TIME available, which of those is better for you?"

FACE-TO-FACE MEETINGS: *"Real-quick, I have your address as ADDRESS, is that correct?"*

TELESALES: *"I just need your email address so that Agent can send you everything and you can see everything in black and white."*

Great, Agent will see/call you at TIME, do you have any other questions for me to let Agent know you were curious about?

Have a nice day!"

CAUTION

The agent should follow any state or federal laws, in addition to any company compliance requirements, pertaining to the need to have assistants licensed or sign HIPPA NDA when approaching leads to qualify, quote, or present plan benefits.

FURTHER YOUR TRAINING

We recommend that agents quickly link up with other agents online to stay current and to constantly improve their sales process. Ways to connect online include LinkedIn Groups and forums. Some forums are free, like The Insurance Forums, whereas some require a paid subscription like, Final Expense 101,[17] Medicare Training 101,[18] Medicare Agent Training,[19] and Final Expense Superstar.[20] These are perhaps the best places to find agents currently sharing what's working best for them, without having to give up any contracts for information and training.

READ MORE BOOKS!

Throughout this book you will see references to other books that have been trailblazers, and we plan to showcase some of the more popular ones on our site in coming months. It's very important that agents immerse themselves in literature of best practices and new ideas, because you never know what technique you may read next that allows you to compound the growth of your business. Whether the book is a classic like Frank Bettger's, "How I Raised Myself From Failure to Success in Selling," or David Duford's "The Official Guide to Selling Final Expense Insurance," or maybe Jeff Root's "The Digital Life Insurance Agent: How to Market Life Insurance

---

[17] https://www.finalexpense101.com/
[18] http://medicaretraining101.com/
[19] http://medicareagenttraining.com/
[20] http://www.finalexpensesuperstar.com/

Online and Sell Over the Phone," these and other books will help any motivated agent quickly become an expert in selling life insurance or Medicare Supplements.

STICKING WITH IT

Selling insurance, like any business, is a marathon, not a sprint. It's as much a mental game of preparing, organizing, and motivating yourself to sell as it is a physical effort of calling, door-knocking, mailing, and reaching out to prospects to turn them into (and keep them onboard as) long-term clients. Making a sale is not an isolated occurrence that happens instantly; it's more often a long, spiraling cycle that requires laying the groundwork to build your business and online brand before even contacting leads, and then following up with clients consistently after a sale to keep them on the books. It requires persistence, endurance, and commitment.

A great, easy-to-read eBook with unique reasons to keep making calls, to keep setting appointments, to keep following up, to keep returning calls, is by Sid Walker. His eBook, "How to Psych Yourself Up to Prospect"[21] is such a simple and elegant reminder of the reasons why we need to keep persevering. Another great book while we are talking about books that make you want to keep going forward is the simple read-it-in-a-day, "Go For No." If you get a chance to read that book it will help you look forward to the rejection that inevitably comes with sales. Perspective is key, without it an agent can lose focus.

RETREAT, REGROUP, REREGISTER

It's not uncommon for a busy, multi-tasking insurance agent to feel burned out at a certain point. Selling can be exhausting! Give yourself a break, if you need to, and then get back on it. Before you give up on your insurance dreams, remind yourself of the reason why you started selling insurance in the first place and remember some of the most memorable, touching, or funny clients you've met

---

[21] http://www.sellingwithoutwrestling.com/psychyourselfupebook.pdf

along the way. These reminders can fuel you toward further sales success.

To make the sales process easier on yourself, consider putting programs and platforms in place that work for you so you don't have to feel overwhelmed doing all of the work for each sale yourself. The next section will explore how to build and maintain an online brand that funnels leads right to you to keep business flowing while you are busy with the usual avenues of lead generation.

PART IV.
ONLINE BRANDING

CHAPTER 11: BUILDING AN ONLINE BRAND

The way agents market and prospect for business is changing. It's challenging to keep up with changes in technology, but the agents who don't evolve with how consumers are now researching and shopping for solutions will have the hardest time finding and keeping clients. Some could argue that this digital reality pertains less to insurance agents who cater to the senior consumer base, saying, "Seniors aren't using computers as much," or, "They don't go on the internet." But the facts betray this outdated stereotype.

- A recent Millward Brown Digital study showed that 42% of baby boomers use a smartphone daily.[22]
- The same study also states that 71% of baby boomers use a tablet or PC daily.

Now, a few agents may point out that baby boomers are just a small piece of the senior population in America; what about the seniors who aren't baby boomers? Baby boomers, who were born between 1946 and 1964, are starting to retire *en masse*. We are only five years into this cresting avalanche of retirees that will be underserved by a similarly retiring population of insurance agents. So what about the other seniors who are older than baby boomers?

A recent Pew study shows that:[23]

- 53% of Americans 65 years and older use the internet or have email.
- 40% of those seniors have broadband service at home.
- 50% of seniors check their email every day.

---

[22] https://www.millwardbrowndigital.com/marketing-to-baby-boomers-dont-ignore-the-pc/

[23] http://www.pewinternet.org/2012/06/06/older-adults-and-internet-use/

- 70% of seniors use the internet daily.

Both the Millward Brown Digital study and the Pew study show that 70% of baby boomers and the older generation of seniors, known as the "Silent Generation," both use the internet on a daily basis. These figures will only grow and the trend will increase until technology is available for every senior to use before making a decision regarding life insurance or Medicare Supplement plans.

Why Do Agents Need to Have an Optimized Online Brand?

Because consumers have an enormous amount of information at their fingertips to consider before making a purchasing decision, it's imperative that agents optimize their online brand so they can cater to this market. Selling insurance used to be so different; without the internet, consumers had to rely on agents for any information to help fix their problems.

Now, consumers can find anything they want to address any problems that plague them, without the need for an agent or salesperson. A recent study by GE Capital Retail Bank[24] found that 79% of consumers feel empowered by technology because it provides them with the necessary information to make an important long-term decision — like finding an affordable Final Expense plan that accepts their health conditions, or finding a company that has a cheaper Medicare Supplement with a more stable rate than they currently pay. The fact that the agent no longer holds the primary dominance when it comes to research before buying decisions is talked about in Joe Pulizzi's book, "Get Content Get Customers," which should be on every agent's book shelf to understand the new online consumer that agents will have to cater to and how to create content that will attract customers in all stages of the buying cycle.

---

[24] https://thornleyfallis.com/81-of-shoppers-research-online-before-buying/

GE Capital Retail Bank's study also shows that at least 81% of consumers do their research before making a financial decision. Some things a senior will research before committing to a Medicare Supplement or Final Expense plan include:

1. **Who is calling them**. Seniors are using the internet to research who's calling them before the agent even gets a chance to present solutions. They're wondering: Is this a salesman, or a call I should answer? Some agents could shoot themselves in the foot by not creating an online brand that takes this crucial first step into consideration.

2. **Agent/agency background**. Some seniors research the agent or agency before they meet with them, or even after they have met. Seniors aren't impulsive decision-makers; some of them prefer to think about the decision or go back online to see what they might have missed. This round of research is usually more intensive than just looking up a cursory number as mentioned above.

3. **Plan details**. Another reason seniors go online to do research is to find out information about the type of plan the agent is recommending. Consumers have a hard time understanding the nuances of insurance. From the types of life insurance coverages (term vs. immediate vs. graded) to the different Medigap plans available (F vs. G vs. N), you can bet that most technologically equipped seniors are researching what you proposed to see if it's the best option available.

4. **Company info**. Seniors head online to research not just the plan but the company issuing the plan. For Final Expense, it's not that big of an issue; the permanent plan is often insured by life insurance "reinsurance pools" that guarantee the plan if the company should ever fail. Unfortunately, if a Medigap company stops issuing a plan in a particular state or altogether, policyholders

may experience rate increases but they don't get a guaranteed issue period to change unless the company itself ceases to exist. Company failure is usually of less concern to seniors than rate stability, which is often their top concern when making a decision to change Medigap plans.

Now that we know without a doubt that seniors are online fact-checking you and your recommendations, it's important to understand that almost 90% of them will consider testimonials and reviews (especially on third-party review sites) when comparing information online. Not only does the agent have to answer any questions that a senior has about him and the products and companies he recommends, but he also has to monitor and cultivate a positive online reputation for his business.

Agents who enhance their online visibility also make themselves more referable. Asking clients for referrals when you have no info on the web can make them feel anxious and unsure — especially if they're newer clients who haven't yet witnessed good customer service or stable rates for their plan. But an agent who has a professional looking website with videos, testimonials (both on the site, in the search engine results, and on third-party review sites), and content that answers common questions or concerns a senior might have about insurance solutions; will earn more business and referrals.

Two Ways to Get Found Online

There are two ways for an agent to get found and develop leads online: pay-per-click (PPC) marketing and organic search engine marketing. One is not necessarily better than the other. However, the majority of insurance agents who don't have exceptionally deep pockets will want to focus more on organic search engine optimization because it's a more solid long-term strategy to get found on the internet — which you cannot say for the pricey yet finite PPC ad campaign.

Search Engine Optimization (SEO) can mean different things to different people. Here are two common interpretations:

- Creating quality content to earn backlinks that will cause you to get more traffic by being found at the top of the search results for certain keywords.
- Building backlinks to pages or blog posts that not only are similar, but offer content to your same audience, which causes the page or post to rank for specific keywords.

Some SEO experts that are purists may tell you only to focus on creating unique content, and the backlinks will come on their own; it's almost a Zen approach to building backlinks. Then there are the "black hat," impatient SEO experts willing to manipulate the search engines into ranking their sites for a certain keyword. They focus more on building backlinks to maneuver into the search engine results than on creating quality content. The ones in the middle are called "grey-hatters," or pragmatic brand builders. They create valuable content *and* find ways to increase the chances of that content earning links to rise in the organic search results for a given keyword or phrase.

A good way to understand the differences between PPC lead generation and SEO lead generation is to check out this video from Rand Fishkin, the founder and CEO of a prominent SEO software company, Moz. He explains to other SEO experts how to position SEO vs. PPC to business owners.[25]

The average agent attempting PPC marketing for the first time will often experience a learning curve that can create a higher lead cost. This is where it's wise to walk before you run. We recommend that agents always diversify their lead sources, but also diversify according to budget and experience instead of jumping into a

---

[25] https://moz.com/blog/make-seo-case-small-businesses-whiteboard-friday

marketing tool blindly. New agents should focus on building a solid foundation for their online brand. The best way to create that solid foundation is first to optimize your brand for organic search results by focusing on SEO; then experiment with PPC lead cultivation.

PPC can be great for creating leads immediately and accessing top-of-the page brand awareness for certain keywords; no one will deny that. But by also cultivating a solid organic SEO strategy for your website, you can bring down the cost of bidding on PPC ads because your well-optimized site will have a higher relevance score for the keywords you are targeting because the PPC bidding system takes this into consideration when calculating the bid amount for each PPC lead.

Four Elements to Building an Online Brand

There are four elements that agents need to focus on to create an viral following for their online brand:

1. Determine appropriate keywords to target.
2. Create a website (we recommend a platform like WordPress).
3. Develop content focused around the keywords you selected that answers typical questions a prospect or client might have regarding Final Expense or Med Supps.
4. Build backlinks to your content to increase brand exposure and your rank in the search results.

The next few chapters will go into these four elements in more detail, but before you start buying a domain and hosting for your new website, you first need to decide which keywords you will target with your website and content. After you know which keywords to target, *then* you can create a website with appropriate content that targets those keywords. We will go over the basics like how many pages you should have on your site and how to create content that can eventually turn prospects into clients.

Finally, this guide will cover the Top Ten forms of backlinks agents can get for their content that will help them build an aura of expertise in their field, display authority, and inspire trust. This guide will also go into some of the precautions when building backlinks that, if ignored, will more than likely get your website labeled as spam and banned from the search results.

Also, at the end of each section there's a "Further Reading" list, like the one below, as resources to help you explore these ideas in more detail. This guide isn't meant to be an instruction manual, but more of a reference manual; listing each area that needs to be considered by agents before they can supplement their prospecting methods with leads from organic search results.

FURTHER READING: SEARCH ENGINE OPTIMIZATION (SEO)

http://neilpatel.com/2016/01/28/how-to-attract-more-local-customers-a-complete-guide-to-local-seo/

http://thesiteedge.com/local-seo-guide/

CHAPTER 12: TARGETING KEYWORDS

Before you can start building pages for your website, or writing content (or outsourcing the writing of it), you have to decide which keywords you will target on those pages. If a website's content incorporates popular keywords, or search terms and phrases that seniors are using, by answering the most pressing questions seniors have about their insurance coverage, it increases the chances that the site will show up higher in the organic search results when someone types in those specific keywords.

TYPES OF KEYWORDS

Just as we recommend diversifying your overall approach to marketing, it's wise to diversify your online keyword strategy by targeting several kinds of keywords to expose your brand or website to the highest potential number of senior readers on the internet. Here are four types of keywords an agent will want to consider when figuring out which keywords to target, in order of the most competitive:

1. **Price Comparison or Buying Keywords:** These are the most actionable keywords to target, and because of that, they come with the most competition. The increased competition, both in organic search engine results and when bidding on PPC ads, happens because these keywords often attract seniors in the ripest buying stage. These are seniors who know their options and just want prices. Examples of these types of keywords include: "Medicare supplement quotes," "New York life insurance quotes," and "cheap term life insurance quotes." These keywords are modified by terms like: "rates," "quotes," and "prices," and contain qualifiers like "cheapest," "best," and "affordable."

2. **General Popular Terms:** These are the general keywords that are very hard to rank for because they're so widely used. However, you should still use these keywords to maintain topical relevance. Examples of these types of keywords include: "burial insurance," "Medigap plans," Medicare Supplement plans," "Medicare," "life insurance," "term life insurance," or "Plan N Medicare Supplement." These keywords and the pages built around them are mostly educational in nature and can be used to generate pillar articles with longer content (more than 1,000 words). These pages will link to other internal pages within your website, which have topical relevance to each particular pillar article. We will cover internal linking later on and why it's important. Also, these terms may draw a ton of traffic, but since the senior isn't in the buying stage and more in the research stage, these keywords will have few buyers associated with them.

3. **State Plan Specific:** These keywords are modified by the name of the state you're working in (or where your target prospects are searching from), along with the type of plan. Some examples include: "New Mexico Medicare Supplements," "burial insurance in Ohio," or "Florida whole life insurance." These keywords, which can have the state before or after the plan, can be quite competitive. But after a year or so of steady SEO, many sites can move into the top ten search results for these types of keywords.

4. **Local Agent/Agency Specific:** To limit keyword competition and find keywords that are easier to rank for than widely used blanket terms like "Final Expense," cast your net a little closer to home and focus on major metropolitan areas or cities where you work. Because these keywords are more specific, like "Baltimore life

insurance agent" or "Indianapolis Medicare agent," they are associated with both lower traffic and lower competition. These keywords usually revolve around a local area, plus a modifier like "agent" or "agency."

For the most part, insurance-related keywords will generally be rather competitive to target because the insurance industry, overall, is a competitive industry when it comes to digital marketing. This is even more so apparent when looking at Aaron Kassover's infographic that shows the average PPC bid for Medicare Supplement keywords.[26] Does that mean a new agent shouldn't try to rank for any keywords? Absolutely not! You should always be creating content on a consistent basis to attract renewals and referrals, in addition to making it easier for potential prospects to find information about you and the solutions you're offering when you contact them initially. Trying to rank for keywords that bring in actual internet leads is a long-term investment that can eventually yield huge dividends to supplement any other prospecting you're doing (more successfully, we hope, after reading this guide).

Selecting Keywords

There are three ways to find out exactly which keywords you should be targeting. The first is to find the websites of your top competitors and put them into Ahref's Site Explorer tool.[27] This paid software tells you what keywords your competitors are ranking for, how much traffic they get from each keyword, which sites are linking to their pages, and more. This Site Explorer tool is by far the gold standard for dissecting and analyzing any competitor's website for a sneak peek into their keyword targeting strategies. The second way to determine which keywords to target

---

[26] http://www.agentmethods.com/infographics/medicare-supplement-and-pay-per-click

[27] https://ahrefs.com/site-explorer

is to buy the pro version of Keyword Tool,[28] a less expensive option than Ahref's Site Explorer tool. Just plug in your state and the type of insurance you sell, and it will bring back a list of keywords, complete with traffic stats and competition for ranking.

The third way to research keywords is the cheapest; in fact, it's free! Just use Google. Head to the search engine, type in your state and the type of insurance you sell — i.e., "Arizona Medicare Supplement," — and scroll to the bottom of the search results page, where you will see other keyword ideas. These alternative phrases or keywords are popular related keyword phrases that seniors are using to find what they are looking for; in this case, Medicare Supplements in Arizona. Click on one of those, and go to the bottom of that search to find even more suggestions.

Of course, there is a fourth way to find keywords, especially if you feel overwhelmed by the whole process — just hire it out. A good SEO company will perform a combination of these methods for you so that you can focus on prospecting and selling. Regardless of how keyword research happens, you should end up with a list of keywords grouped together in various categories for relevance. A Medicare Supplement agent wouldn't have keywords targeting life insurance on his Medicare Supplement page, and likewise, a Final Expense agent shouldn't use keywords targeting "term life insurance" on pages about buying burial insurance.

However, "term life insurance" may be an applicable LSI keyword for a Final Expense agent to acknowledge on a page about aged life insurance leads. After selecting your primary keywords, you'll also want to look at related LSI keywords, which stands for Latent Semantic Indexing. LSI keywords are closely related terms and phrases (not limited to synonyms) that show up frequently along with other primary keywords that tell the search engines what topic the content is about. For example, if a page has

---

[28] http://www.keywordtool.io/

information about life insurance, chances are it will use related terms like *term life insurance, PHI, underwriting, guaranteed rates,* and *tax-free death benefit.* Likewise, a page about Medigap plans in Indiana may contain similar LSI keywords like *Plan F, CMS, open enrollment,* and *Medicare Part B deductible.* Search engines can tell what is topically relevant by comparing keywords with other LSI keywords.

Content that contains primary keywords from the categories we covered above, along with any corresponding LSI keywords, will have a higher chance of ranking for a given keyword because it builds context and relevance. The easiest way to find LSI keywords is through the website, www.LSIGraph.com. Use their free tool to find terms related to your target keywords to add into your pages' content. This tool can also give you some great ideas to develop content for your blog.

How to Target Keywords

Just repeating keywords across the entire website or page will not help you rank for them. An ideal keyword frequency is to have the keyword you're targeting show up no more than 1.5% of the time. More than that may turn off readers because it's hard to make a higher keyword density be readable without sounding repetitive. If you go overboard and "stuff" the keyword into your content, not only will you potentially lose readers, but search engines may even penalize the website, knocking you out of the search results altogether.

Search engines like Google don't just look at the keyword itself or how often it's used; they also look to see where keywords are located on the page, ascribing more weight to words placed in prominent positions, such as:

1. In the page title
2. In the first header

3. In the first paragraph
4. In the conclusion
5. Anywhere else in the body of the content that may be appropriate

For a better look at what an optimized page looks like, read Backlinko's guide to on-page SEO by Brian Dean.[29]

Regardless of how you research or select your keywords, you have to target all four types of keywords to:

1. Be found locally (bonus: local searches are the easiest to rank for!)
2. Build content around actionable or "buying" keywords to capture prospects who may be ready to look at options whether they found you organically or not.
3. Build content around general terms to help educate seniors in the "information-seeking" phase of the buying cycle.
4. Develop your site into an overall authority on the subject, gradually competing with higher competition phrases as you start to rank for lower competition phrases.

Let's talk about the fourth reason in more detail. Both Brian Dean of Backlinko and Chris Lee of RankXL talk about the importance of ranking for lower competition keywords first. It's well documented that sites ranking high for lower competition keywords also rank higher for other keywords they target, whether those are high- or low-competition. Because it's easier to rank for keywords with less competition, low-competition keywords can help new websites become authorities on their subject in the eyes

---

[29] http://backlinko.com/on-page-seo

of the search engine, which will give the site an extra boost for other keywords it's targeting (even more competitive ones). This should encourage agents that, by slowly but surely building content and links to your site, you keep increasing your authority, enabling you to eventually rank for keywords against higher competition.

FURTHER READING: KEYWORD RESEARCH

https://ahrefs.com/blog/keyword-research/

https://www.brightlocal.com/2014/07/22/effective-local-keyword-research/

http://seopressor.com/blog/how-to-do-local-keyword-research-for-your-local-business/

http://www.advancedwebranking.com/blog/google-didnt-want-us-to-use-the-keyword-planner-this-way/

CHAPTER 13: CREATING A WEBSITE

Just as "a journey of a thousand miles begins with a single step," the never-ending process of creating (and maintaining) a website begins with five critical pages that construct the foundation of your online presence. Of course, before you even buy a domain or initiate this process, you should already understand what your site will be about, after considering which keywords to target like we discussed in the previous chapter.

The most important pages that an agent needs to create on his website before he can start promoting his brand online include:

- About Us page
- Contact Us page
- Privacy Policy page
- Terms of Service page
- Homepage / Landing page(s)

The **About Us** page should be a minimum of 500 to 750 words, covering the basic information that a prospect or client would want to know about your business, like:

- How long you have been in business
- Any community charitable causes you support
- Competitive differences between you and your competition
- Mission statements, core values, or goals

This is where you can tell the story of why you started selling insurance or explain the history behind your company. Mention any relevant local communities, associations, events, or places to illustrate that you're a servant of the local community. Be sure to include a picture of yourself and any applicable staff, and a photo of your agency or office, if possible. This type of info produces transparency and trust with site visitors by introducing the professionals who will be helping them with their insurance needs.

The **Contact Us** page should, at a minimum, share the agent's (or agency's) Name, Address, and Phone number (N.A.P.). It's wise to also include this information prominently on your homepage, allowing visitors to call or email you with one click, in addition to providing this key basic information on a dedicated Contact page. Include your full physical address; in fact, it's best to embed a Google Map of your location to further reinforce the credibility of your professional brick-and-mortar business. If you're an independent agent who works out of your home, then you have a few options that we'll cover in a little bit.

The **Contact Us** page should include a contact form with the minimum fields:

1. Name
2. Email
3. Reason for contacting you

You can make this a full-fledged quote form with plan-specific check-marked options, mandatory phone number fields, etc. However, the more fields you put on your contact form, the less often someone will fill it out entirely, so it's important to only request the most pertinent information. Consumers are still more likely to call a phone number listed at the top at the top of a website, or to use an email address if one is listed prominently, than to fill out a contact form. Be sure your phone number and email are displayed at the top of your website so your contact info shows up on every page!

Only prospects who are looking for specific quotes or rates will bother to fill out a longer quote form, but this may scare off people who just have preliminary questions but aren't yet ready to buy. Ultimately, it's up to agents to decide if they want their contact form to be a quote form — or if they want to make two separate pages. Some agents have one general N.A.P. contact page, usually linked in the primary navigation bar at the top of the website, and then they place a banner ad at the top of the site that visitors can click when they're ready to request a quote, that will take them to a specific page where they can input more info to get specific rates and quotes back. Either option is fine as long as the form isn't too cumbersome and easy to find.

A **Privacy Policy** page and **Terms of Service** page are two pages that, while necessary, will be used more by search engines to indicate that you are a legitimate business than they will be used by the average consumer visiting your site. These links are usually tucked in the footer at the bottom of the homepage. The majority of website owners just use a template version; a great example is www.termsfeed.com, where you can create a template version for free. Of course, we encourage agents to check with their attorneys regarding any legal documentation like this.

LANDING PAGES

The last type of page that's imperative to an agent's website is a Landing Page that encompasses four major areas:

1. Products Sold
2. Problems Solved
3. People Helped
4. Areas Served

The landing page might be the homepage, especially if you only sell one type of insurance. If you sell multiple types of insurance, your homepage should list the types of insurance you sell, and link each one to separate pages that discuss each type of insurance. Then each of those separate pages would be its own landing page.

Unbounce, one of the leading authorities on this topic, defines "a landing page as being **a standalone web page distinct from your main website** that has been designed for a single focused objective." In this case, the focus is having the prospect fill out a quote or contact form on an individual product the agent offers that solves a particular problem for seniors. A Final Expense agent will have a landing page centered around permanent life insurance, while a Medicare Supplement agent will have a landing page devoted strictly to Medicare Supplement plans the agent offers or recommends. If you target different states on one website, you can have landing pages focused on each state, and possibly sub-landing pages for each type of insurance in each state. If you go that route, you'll have to create unique content for each page. For more on content, keep reading the next chapter where we dive more in-depth into that.

CAUTION

Pages with light content or repetitive content will be penalized and possibly blocked from the search engine results or, even worse, the search engine may send security warnings to browsers indicating potential spam associated with the site.

There are numerous landing page templates an agent can use; some of them can be pretty fancy. A superior landing page will include these elements:

1. Contact info displayed prominently at the top right of the page, featuring a local phone number and a toll-free number (a local one works best).
2. A video, if possible, which helps decrease bounce rate, increase trust, and establish authority.
3. A quote form for prospects who are interested in this particular product.
4. A list of problems the product helps seniors solve.
5. The agent's process for responding, i.e. "We'll call within 24 hours of receiving your quote request," "You'll only be contacted by one agent dedicated to you," or, "One of our agents will follow up with you within 48 hours to answer any questions you have."
6. A possible testimonial from a client who has benefitted from this product.

PAGE CONTENT

After the agent has a list of landing pages with appropriate keywords that they will target, he can begin to create content for these pages. Insurance content needs to revolve around two main concepts: the problems seniors have, and the insurance plans that can solve those problems. That's the basic formula for insurance content. Whether you use graphics, videos, case studies, testimonials, or informative articles to accentuate this content depends on the skill, budget, and time you have.

The easiest way to find out what kind of content to write about is to see what's already working for other successful sites. Browse through competitors' sites to check out their content; pay attention to what you like and what you could do better. A smart content strategy includes an analysis of the top 10-20 search results for each keyword that a landing page targets. Note the different topics each page covers, what points they try to make. Compile all of these points together and rewrite it in your language, adding examples from your experience, to make sure the content is unique.

The best thing you can do when creating content is to put yourself in the senior's shoes and imagine what information a senior would need, or questions he would ask, before choosing a Medicare Supplement or Final Expense insurance plan.

A great resource to help with this process is the site www.answerthepublic.com, where you can input various keywords (for free) to see popular questions people are asking about that topic. Incorporate those questions and answers into the content topics you find from your competitors, and you'll have an extensive list of ideas for your website.

Lastly, look for statistics from other authority websites that can support your content. Not only does this lend credibility to your writing from the reader's perspective, but using statistics and linking to high-authority websites is a clear signal to search engines like Google that your website is using reliable information and trying to produce value by linking to other valuable websites. A Final Expense agent will link to sites like LIMRA[30] and other authoritative sites like www.LifeHappens.org.[31] Medicare Supplement agents should link to www.medicare.gov, their state's insurance website, or www.ssa.gov. Linking to authoritative sites like ones above, signal to the search engines that "you are trying to provide your site visitors with rich content designed to solve problems and answer questions, if that means going to another site to find it, so be it!" This act of selflessness in the eyes of the search engines inspires a lot of trust and helps the site rank better for keywords.

---

[30] http://www.limra.com/

[31] http://www.lifehappens.org/

MOBILE OPTIMIZATION

An important requirement many website owners have dealt with lately is how their site shows up on mobile browsers, also known as mobile optimization. Google recently changed its search algorithms to de-emphasize websites that aren't optimized for both desktop and mobile devices. In Google's eyes, the future is centered around mobile technology, and with seniors using technology in increasing fashion, it's crucial for agents to make sure their sites are optimized appropriately.

If you use a WordPress website, you simply download the Jetpack plugin, check the mobile theme box under settings, and it will optimize your site automatically for mobile searches. If you don't have a WordPress site, you'll have to find an alternative software option or even hire a developer to build a mobile site.

Now that you have an idea of what pages you need and which keywords they are targeting, let's cover how to produce some unique and interesting content in order to remain relevant and useful to your audience.

FURTHER READING: WEBSITE AND LANDING PAGE CREATION

https://www.quicksprout.com/landing-page-optimization/

https://moz.com/blog/most-entertaining-guide-to-landing-page-optimization

https://yoast.com/wordpress-seo/

http://www.viperchill.com/wordpress-seo/

https://codeable.io/wordpress-seo-tips-guide/

CHAPTER 14: DEVELOPING CONTENT

After you create your website, starting with the first five pages and other foundational factors we discussed in the last few chapters, the next step is to build your website into an authority by establishing your expertise, promoting your brand, and building relationships.

Your ability to do this depends on the content you develop for your website. Simply writing about a few insurance keywords and slapping them up on your website does not make you an authority. Writing and publishing pages and posts is not the end goal of developing content for your website because, of course, you want to make sure that what you write gets read.

You shouldn't be writing content just to write; you should be more concerned about writing strategic content that people actually want to read. Sure, content is an important tool in itself because it allows you to give your business a voice and illustrate your unique perspective, while keeping your website from looking bare or barely visited. But ultimately, the goal of your content isn't just to *exist;* you want your content to drive action from readers by convincing them to request a quote on the Final Expense plan you so eloquently described, or to sign up for your email newsletter because your blog post about the latest changes to Medicare was so helpful.

Before your content can accomplish anything for your business, though, it has to get found first. You can encourage this by trying to obtain links from other websites that link back to a specific page on your website. These backlinks reinforce a website's value with the search engines by proving that other sites find its content valuable enough to link to. Basically, links give your content a vote of approval by saying that it's worth sharing.

Having these links doesn't necessarily catapult a website to No. 1 in the search engine results; just ask any impatient website owner who has been burned by buying tens of thousands of links very cheaply, with no measurable impact on ranking. Links can come from a multitude of different websites, and not all links have the same value because not all websites have the same authority or quality of content. Websites that happen to have a lot of links pointing to them usually have amazing and engaging content that keeps readers on site longer to read more pieces of content, compared to another website ranking lower in the search engines. A site with lots of links indicates to Google or other search engines that its content is valuable enough that people are linking to it, suggesting that it deserves a higher rank in the results when people search for that particular keyword or phrase.

You must have helpful, shareable content to earn these links, so the site moves up the search engine ranks, to earn more exposure and more leads. This means that just setting up a bare-bones site with the minimum pages we covered in the last chapter isn't enough. You must create content that engages site visitors enough to turn them into leads, and then to turn those leads into clients, and then to turn your clients into raving, referring fans. Your content should cater to seniors at every stage of the consumer buying cycle, which according to Hubspot,[32] spans:

1. Curiosity or awareness of a problem
2. Researching options
3. Comparing prices
4. Signing up
5. Re-evaluating purchase decisions.

---

[32] https://blog.hubspot.com/blog/tabid/6307/bid/19022/How-to-Leverage-the-5-Stages-of-the-Customer-Buying-Cycle-for-More-Sales.aspx

When agents have volumes of quality content to address a variety of questions that the average senior may have throughout every stage of the sales cycle, then the chances of their site being found by someone — particularly, by someone who considers the site a resource worthy of sharing or linking — increases exponentially.

Jon Ball wrote an article for Search Engine Land about the top reasons why website owners (or, in our case, agents) would want to obtain links.[33] The three top reasons from the article, in our opinion, are increasing search engine visibility, increasing brand exposure, followed by building relationships. In other words, links provide the juice or fuel that powers your content to get it in front of prospects.

Writing relevant and engaging content that's good enough to earn links from other high-traffic and relevant websites will:

- Help the agent look like an expert, which makes it easier to partner up with other websites to promote your brand.
- Lend authority to the website, which will expand the chances of being found online for any keywords the website's content targets.
- Build trust in any potential prospects who are visiting the website for research.
- Make the agent more referable and his brand more reputable.

But to earn links, the agent must first write quality content worth sharing. Linkable content displays these traits:

- Readable and not jargon-heavy

[33] http://searchengineland.com/build-links-6-reasons-link-building-2014-193279

- Valuable because it conveys ideas in a graspable manner that benefits the reader
- Uses keywords in appropriate areas on the page
- Lengthy, as long as 1,000-2,500 words or more
- Uses graphics in the form of videos, pictures, or charts that help visually explain points
- Answers readers' questions
- Can be easily viewed from either a desktop or mobile device
- Shareable from a social media standpoint

Neil Patel, a popular digital marketer, has a great guide[34] on creating linkable content to build an aura of expertise, which can inspire trust in prospects and clients to increase the number of:

- Calls taken or returned
- Appointments kept
- Frequency of sales
- Referrals earned or obtained

SAY IT DIFFERENTLY

Creating content that answers consumers' questions about insurance while explaining their options is key. Browsing other sites to find articles about your keywords can give you some topic ideas to tackle this. But the main content quandary is that many of your potential topics have probably been written about before. Creating content that is new and refreshing and adds a fresh perspective is particularly challenging, especially in a technical

---

[34] https://www.quicksprout.com/the-advanced-guide-to-content-marketing-chapter-1/

industry like insurance. No one wants to read the 31,801st article on "term vs. whole life insurance," but if you can add a metaphor to the conversation that no one has talked about before, or if you put it in a different format like a clever infographic, then the chances of your content being read, enjoyed, and linked to increases dramatically. Additional formats you may want to use to educate seniors about insurance include:

1. **Video:** One of the most powerful forms of content, video is a widely consumed, highly compelling medium to provide education. The agent who can create entertaining videos, especially about topics that aren't inherently entertaining, will become a highly regarded expert in no time. Video can literally put a face and personality to your content. Another benefit of utilizing video is that it can bypass text-only content in organic search results and show up first, if the video has been properly optimized.

2. **Infographics:** This can be a somewhat expensive format requiring the agent to work with a graphic designer and come up with an idea to illustrate numerical data and interesting stats in a visually entertaining way. A simple search for Medicare or life insurance infographics will give you plenty of ideas to start with. You can also make infographics yourself by searching for "free infographic creator" and utilizing the free tools and templates found on each site; more than 50 templates appear in the top ten search results.

3. **Pictures:** Pictures can lend context and meaning to your written content, explain it in visual terms, or break up the text to improve readability — all of which will increase the value of that content. Pictures, like videos, can sometimes show up above the organic search results

if they are properly optimized for the keywords they depict.

4. **Sound:** Agents who utilize audio recordings or podcasts can slowly build an online following by consistently creating new content. A popular podcast example for life insurance is "The Insurance Pro Blog," where they dissect and thoroughly analyze everything related to insurance, mostly permanent insurance. This is a great way to be perceived as an expert and authority in your field.

5. **eBook:** Agents who want to build instant credibility should consider writing an eBook (or hiring a content agency[35] to help you organize and polish your thoughts). An eBook can be used as a lead magnet to entice site visitors to sign up for your monthly newsletter in exchange for a copy of your eBook. This type of long-form content can be used to educate leads in early stages of the buying cycle, while establishing trust with seniors in the later stages of the buying cycle.

CONTENT THAT GOOGLE WILL "EAT" UP

Recently, Google came out with new guidelines for writing content that has the potential to impact "a person's financial health." This means that agents and insurance companies have an extra duty to write credible content using accurate information to help readers make wise financial decisions. Google's new content requirements are often referred to as **EAT** because they outline the importance of writing content that establishes **Expertise**, **Authority**, and **Trust**. Google considers these the top three requirements for content that could affect someone's financial health:

---

[35] http://www.bantamedia.com/

- **EXPERTISE**: This requirement is reflected in the need for content to be written by a professional or expert within the field. This means that bloggers or site owners need to enlist the aid of an expert in the field they are writing about (which may be an opportunity for you to partner up with bloggers and lend your expertise to a larger audience). It also means that agents who write their own content need to be viewed as experts in their field, which requires each agent to have an online brand that reflects his expertise. If you don't have social media profiles, online bios, and a website cross-promoting your content, then Google gives your brand less emphasis when ranking your site.

- **AUTHORITY:** This requirement centers around the site being a valuable, well-rounded source of information that provides resources for readers while connecting to other authoritative sites to lend value and educate consumers. This means agents must find other sites and resources to link to within the content they develop. Site owners who don't link out will lose rankings because linking from your content to other valuable, relevant content shows Google that your site is acting like an authority on the subject and attempting to deliver credible information to readers.

- **TRUST:** A website is considered more trustworthy if it exhibits some or all of the following 10 requirements:

    1. Layout is organized logically, with minimal ads and no deceptive advertising.

    2. Contact information is clearly listed on the site.

    3. Privacy policy and terms of service pages are listed somewhere on the site.

4. The brand is established with business citation backlinks.

5. Site includes mentions from media and other local organizations.

6. Bounce rate is low, meaning people stay on the site longer because they're finding appropriate and valuable content.

7. Site is optimized for mobile browsers.

8. Pages aren't deemed to have "light content," less than 750 words.

9. Site doesn't have spammy, low-quality, or low-traffic backlinks.

10. Anchor text isn't overly optimized for a particular keyword (which will be explained later on in the backlink chapter.)

If the agent can inspire trust on his website and within his content, address all the relevant topics like an authority site would do, and cross-promote his content and brand like an expert, then his site is much more likely to rank for the keywords he's targeting. Insurance content deals with topics that have the potential to affect the financial health and decision-making of readers; that means these **EAT** requirements are critical — not just for the sake of your site ranking, but for the sake of your potential and existing clients!

The key rule to writing content that makes Google happy (though the specific rules and algorithms change frequently) is to focus on writing content that makes your readers (prospects and/or clients) happy by answering their questions thoroughly in an interesting or entertaining way while keeping them on the site.

Part of your job as an insurance agent is to provide accurate information to help your prospects and clients make decisions, and your website is one of the best places to do it. Not only are insurance agents being required to act more like fiduciaries in financial matters, as illustrated by the Department of Labor ruling, but Google requires agents to act like fiduciaries when writing content, as well. The agent who can produce content that is engaging and also satisfies the EAT requirements can effectively build an online brand that converts traffic into clients, inspire trust from prospects, and become more referable in clients' eyes — all with higher search rankings, of course.

FURTHER READING: CONTENT CREATION

https://www.quicksprout.com/the-advanced-guide-to-content-marketing/

https://moz.com/blog/indepth-guide-to-content-creation-with-infographic

http://webris.org/content-marketing/creation/

https://blog.hubspot.com/marketing/free-content-marketing-tools-list/

https://www.sitepoint.com/ultimate-guide-link-building-content/

CHAPTER 15: BUILDING LINKS & PROMOTING YOUR BRAND

As we explained in the last chapter, links are the fuel that helps your content get in front of online traffic. In an article for Moz,[36] an authoritative website for everything related to Search Engine Optimization (SEO), digital marketer Paddy Moogan describes what exactly a link is and how link building works:

> *"Link building is the process of acquiring hyperlinks from other websites to your own. A hyperlink (usually just called a link) is a way for users to navigate between pages on the internet. Search engines use links to crawl the web; they will crawl the links between the individual pages on your website, and they will crawl the links between entire websites."*

Although search engines may be crawling links to, from, and within your site to determine what your content is about and when to feature it in search results, don't think that you can game the system by obtaining (or buying) a huge amount of links to trick the search engines or boost your rank. Matt Cutts, a software engineer at Google, explains that *any* manipulation of links to increase a site's rank on search engine results is forbidden and "unnatural." Google doesn't want to see people just getting links for the sake of getting links; they want site owners to cultivate legitimate brands that provide value, unique perspective, and service — not just run websites that build a lot of links. What Google wants to see is websites trying to earn links naturally by creating informative content that other websites want to share.

[36] https://moz.com/beginners-guide-to-link-building

The top three questions agents should ask themselves when considering if they should pursue obtaining a link with another website is:

A. **Does the site have topical relevance?** A site about Medicare or life insurance is very topically relevant. A website with content aimed at the same audience that the agent is prospecting (baby boomers and other seniors), like a site devoted to senior health issues or a site for retirees, is slightly topically relevant. A website about insurance in general, like auto and home insurance, would be considered even less relevant. The goal when building links is to connect with other sites that are relevant to both the audience the agent serves and the types of insurance he sells.

B. **Does the site have traffic?** You could get a link to your website listed on an agent directory, but what's the value of being listed on a site if the site isn't optimized or promoted to reach your audience — or anyone at all? No traffic means no value; it means the site isn't creating content that is helpful for site visitors, or actively promoting it. The goal is to build links with high-traffic sites that get you in front of as many eyes as possible.

C. **Is it easy to get a link?** The easier it is to get a link from a site, generally, the less value the link holds in the eyes of the search engines. For instance, anyone can get a citation from Google by having a Google My Business page; just having this link by itself doesn't necessarily convey authority (although it's still good for Local SEO), but having a guest post on a top Medicare website, and a link from a particular state's department of insurance, and being featured in the news as an expert or authority on the subject, are considered much harder to obtain and even more valuable in the eyes of the search engines.

Even if you're successful in accumulating backlinks to the pages on your website, you won't automatically see your rank increase on search engine results for a specific keyword or multiple keywords overnight. It takes almost ten weeks, on average, to start seeing results, according to SEO manager Kristina Kledzik in an article for Moz.[37]

Listed below are eight of the most common ways agents can obtain links and increase traffic to their website. Of course, you want your site to have a variety of links; a site only focusing on one linking method could potentially look unnaturally deliberate and spammy to the search engines.

On the other hand, you don't want to overdo your links, either. Every linking method below can be abused, but if the content is valuable, unique, informative, and entertaining, and if the referring or linking site isn't using unethical or "black hat" methods, then the link will not be considered spammy.

For each linking method listed below, we describe the method and explain the quality of the link building method itself, in addition to some tools that can help you with the process. After each backlink method, we'll provide Further Reading links to explain and teach each method in more depth.

1. BUSINESS CITATIONS

Business citations are any mentions of you or your company's name, address, and phone number (N.A.P.) online. Citations may just list this basic info, or they may also be accompanied by a link to your website. Citations can either be structured (meaning the site offers a dedicated place to put your information, like a GMB page, a Facebook business page, a social media profile, or a review-based profile like on Yelp) or unstructured (meaning your info appears within the content of a web page, potentially alongside other

[37] https://moz.com/blog/how-long-does-link-building-take-influence-rankings

business listings, like in a blog post, a social media update, or in a blog comment in response to someone's question: "Does anyone know a good insurance agent that deals with Medicare plans in Oregon?")

An agent can also sign up with various listings or directories (national or local) that funnel interested prospects to local agents. Citations signal that the business or professional listed is legitimate. N.A.P. mentions "help increase the degree of certainty the search engines have about your business's contact information," as noted on Moz.

It's critical to be consistent with every mention and every citation of your business on the internet. One of the largest factors for websites ranking locally (or not ranking at all) is "N.A.P. Consistency." If your business is listed on Manta with a different name, address, or phone number — even with the slightest variation, like Associates vs. Assoc. in your name or Street vs. St. in your address — any difference is enough to draw scrutiny in the eyes of the search engines. That's why it's important for agents to perform citation audits to maintain consistency.

There are hundreds of citation sources for U.S. businesses, depending on the location and type of business. There are also four major data aggregators (F.A.I.L.) that filter their information into national citation sources. These big four data aggregators are:

- Factual
- Acxiom
- Infogroup
- Localeze

In addition to these four data aggregators, an agent has even more citation possibilities when including local or state geographical areas, like your metropolitan newspaper's online business directory, as well as national insurance industry sites like the National Association of Health Underwriters agent directory (www.nahu.org). A list of common business citations can be found in the Further Reading section below.

Verifying that your business's N.A.P. info is accurate on all four data aggregators, any relevant local or national directories, and on your branded social media accounts gives you a greater chance of getting your business into Google's data warehouse known as the Knowledge Graph. Having a Knowledge Graph info box show up when someone searches your name or agency is a true hallmark of a professional, stable business.

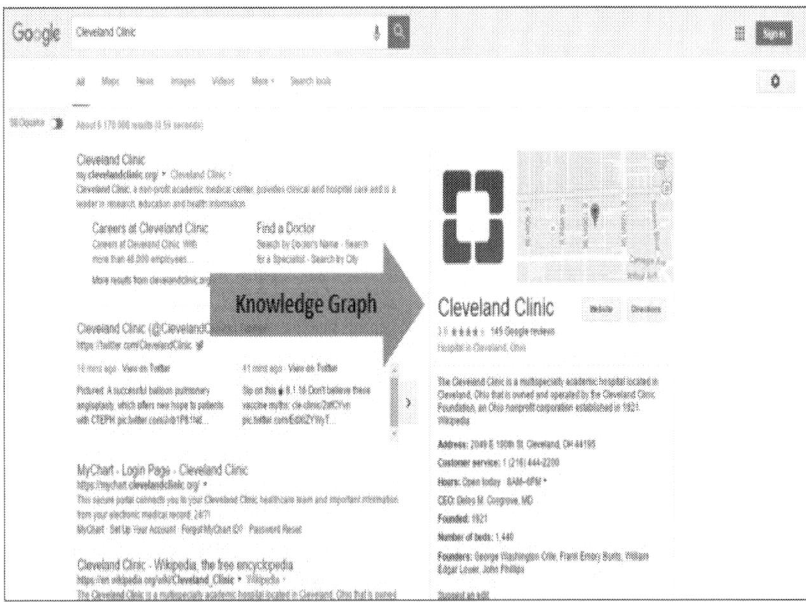

Ways to Create Citations

You have three options for increasing the number of citations your business has: create the citations yourself (perhaps with the help of an employee or assistant), hire the work out to a search engine optimization company, or enlist the aid of a citation building website like BrightLocal[38] or Whitespark.[39]

Creating the citations yourself is the cheapest route, but it takes quite a bit of time to create accounts, verify them, fill in every content field (uniquely), add pictures, etc. If you use a website to create the citations for you, make sure to read the fine print; some will take down the citation if you stop paying the monthly subscription price. You'll pay more to outsource citation building to an agency that specializes in SEO, but at least it will be done correctly and professionally. You might spend anywhere from $3-$7 per citation, depending on quality and quickness, but at least you're assured that they won't be taken down later on (be sure to read your SEO agency's contract!)

FURTHER READING: CITATIONS

http://www.omnicoreagency.com/local-seo-citation-sources-usa/

https://whitespark.ca/top-local-citation-sources-by-country/

https://www.brightlocal.com/2015/03/31/local-citation-sites-for-top-100-usa-cities/

https://moz.com/blog/advanced-citation-audit-clean-up-achieve-consistent-data-higher-rankings

https://incomebully.com/local-seo-citation-building-guide/

38 https://www.brightlocal.com/
39 https://whitespark.ca/

2. SOCIAL MEDIA AND WEB 2.0

A Web 2.0 site is any site that allows users to add content to the site, whether it's their own or someone else's. These may include blogs (WordPress, Blogger), wikis (Wikipedia, wikiHow, Wikisource.org), social bookmarking sites (Reddit, Delicious, StumbleUpon, Scoop.it), and social media sites like Facebook, Google Plus, Pinterest, or LinkedIn where you can share status updates, links, and other posts. Social media links are a type of Web 2.0 links, but they are often distinguished separately because they have the effect of representing the brand more directly. Due to the importance of these websites, it's best to put them in a category of their own aside from other 2.0 sites.

SECURE YOUR BRAND

By setting up accounts and filling out your info on social media and other Web 2.0 sites, you begin to secure your brand online across many properties and platforms that point back to your site with backlinks to boot! Brand securitization is the process of claiming your "brand real estate" on these sites. This does three major things:

1. Prevents competitors from taking up possible brand-related names or, even worse, hijacking them with an inappropriate or inconsistent messages.

2. Expands your brand onto other sites where you can share valuable content, whether you created it yourself or curated it from another noteworthy source.

3. Helps manage your online reputation because these high-traffic sites can make up the top search results for you or your agency's name.

The first and most important step in securing your brand and developing an online business persona is creating a Google My Business (GMB) page for your business. If you have a brick-and-mortar office, you should create a location page to display your street address. If you work from home (unless you receive clients at your home office), choose a service area page instead; there is also an option to keep your address private if you choose. Generally, the best option is a brick-and-mortar location because it gives the agent a higher chance of ranking for what's called the "3-pack," which is the top 3 local businesses that rank for a certain local keyword. These show up in prime digital real estate underneath the pay-per-click ads and above the organic search results.

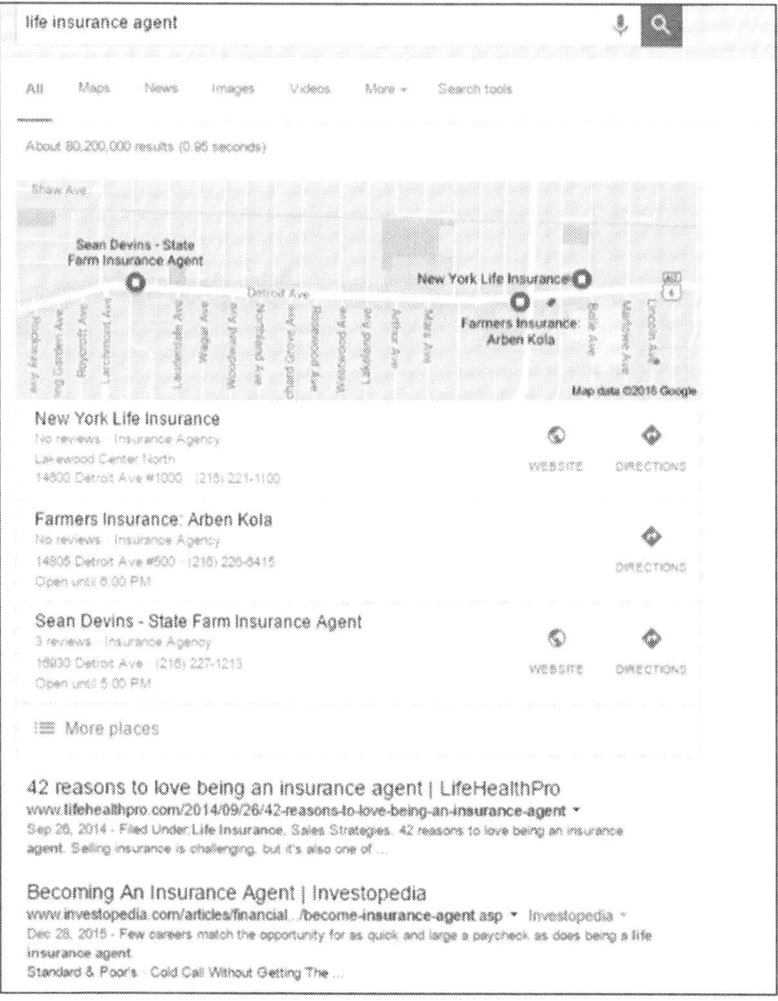

Set up social media channels like your Facebook business page, LinkedIn, Pinterest, Instagram, and Twitter, by filling out information completely and optimizing the pictures and contact information for each channel. After you set up the channels, maintain your presence there by posting content regularly. An agent has three options when it comes to sharing content on social media channels:

1. Create content on the site to share (status update, post, etc.)

2. Share content you created either on your site or someone else's (guest post)

3. Curate news updates from other sites to maintain topical **top-of-mind expert status**

Develop a social media posting schedule to keep these channels populated with a fresh mix of content. Social media dashboards like Hootsuite allow you to schedule posts in advance across multiple channels. This is perhaps the most useful free social media tool an agent can use to make sure he has some piece of content, whether curated or created, to share on those channels consistently. The advantage of having a social media dashboard that promotes scheduled posting (like Hootsuite) is that it allows the agent to:

1. Devote less time to posting on social media channels

2. Stay topical by sharing the latest industry news, helping you appear as an expert

3. Display online professionalism by having consistent social media posts instead of infrequently posting and then dropping it only to pick it up again months down the line.

How to Use Social Media 2.0 Sites

Websites that allow users to generate content or link to other content are possible link opportunities that agents can pursue for their web pages and blog posts to get the word out. Dhiraj Das, writing on SourceWP,[40] listed more than 250 sites that are good to pursue links from. Anytime the agent creates valuable content, whether it's a blog post, an infographic, or a podcast, he will want to share it on some of these sites to earn the page or post backlinks — which may even cause the content to go viral if enough people see it and share it, which could earn the agent's site even more backlinks.

Courting Reviews and Online Reputation Management

Securing your brand across hundreds of possible websites not only builds a foundation for your brand to become known by broadcasting content through various outlets, but it helps you control the top search results that show up for your name or agency. This helps to mitigate potential online reputation issues that pop up with negative reviews stemming from irate clients, internet trolls, or more than likely— competitors.

In addition to securing your brand online, agents should be proactive in courting reviews from clients. Consumers can leave reviews of insurance agents on their Google page, Facebook page, LinkedIn page, etc. An insurance agent who courts testimonials by channeling their clients to the appropriate review site can yield massive dividends when prospects are researching an agent's reputation, or when clients are considering referring the agent to others.

---

[40] https://www.sourcewp.com/free-dofollow-social-bookmarking-sites-list

You can also print out or send directions to clients explaining how to leave reviews on review sites. This will help the agent cultivate:

- An online following
- A positive online reputation
- More referrals from clients

CAUTION

One word of warning to agents when it comes to asking clients for online reviews: It's best not to prompt senior clients to create an account just to review your services. To a review site, seeing a new account review a single business looks like a possible fake or spam account created to boost reviews. There are two things an agent can do to avoid this: either prompt seniors to review some other local businesses nearby when they review yours if their account is new, or ask seniors if they have an account with a particular site i.e. Google, Facebook, etc., then give them the appropriate instructions to leave a review on that particular site(s).

A great handout to give to clients to have them review your services online is Phil Rozek's form.[41]

Insurance agents wishing to strategically seek out reviews could enlist the help of a Review Funnel, which depending on the software, can not only filter reviews and mitigate complaints, but also help display reviews on your website like the popular Review

[41] https://whitespark.ca/review-handout-generator/

Funnel company Grade.us.[42] Another review funnel that agents might think about is Feedback Magnet.[43]

FURTHER READING: SOCIAL MEDIA

https://incomebully.com/the-ultimate-guide-to-using-parasites-for-seo-and-more

https://blog.hootsuite.com/how-to-use-social-video-for-marketing/

http://neilpatel.com/what-is-social-media-marketing/

https://blog.hootsuite.com/the-essential-guide-to-social-media-marketing/

https://brandyourself.com/online-reputation-management

3. Blog Comments

Blog commenting is one of those outdated SEO techniques that many new and aspiring marketers trip over in their attempts to attract easy backlinks. The truth about blog commenting is that it is more valuable as a networking tool or to funnel traffic to your website and network with other blog owners, than it is as a backlink meant to optimize your site for a given keyword or topic in the search results.

Commenting on blogs is an old classic that has the potential to help agents who know how to use it wisely. Of course, you want to choose an appropriate blog or article that covers topics relevant to your site, like Medicare, life insurance, funeral planning, retirement, or senior health care.

---

[42] https://www.grade.us/home

[43] https://feedbackmagnet.com/

COMPLETE THE PROFILE FIRST

To utilize this technique to the fullest, start by developing a brand profile for the blog commenting format, whether on WordPress, Disqus, or an individual industry (ProducersWeb[44]) or news website (LifeHealthPro,[45] InsuranceNewsNet[46]). Use your first and last name (or last initial), and fill out the profile with a professional looking picture. If there's a place to include your website, do so for a profile backlink (low in quality, but still a backlink).

WEB-ETIQUETTE

Once your profile is ready for commenting, consider the web-etiquette that should be followed when commenting and leaving backlinks. Sites handle comments with backlinks differently: some comments will be moderated out, and some will be allowed. It usually depends on the quality of the comment, if you add value by contributing good points that you agree with (especially ones you have written about and want to link to) to illustrate the blog topic further, then that is perfectly acceptable. An agent can even disagree with the author, providing he is polite and has solid reasons to support his argument.

What usually isn't acceptable is name-calling, critiquing without proper reasoning, short content responses that don't reference the article, or leaving a backlink that doesn't further illustrate the author's stance or your reasoning for disagreement.

USING BLOG COMMENTING TO BUILD RELATIONSHIPS AND PROMOTE CONTENT

If you're going to comment on other blogs, pick blogs with authors who are influencers within:

[44] http://www.producersweb.com

[45] http://www.lifehealthpro.com/

[46] http://www.insurancenewsnet.com/

A. Insurance industry

B. Senior health care industry (for Med Supp agents)

C. Local communities surrounding you (or your clients)

D. Websites centered around retirement

E. Journalists for news and media that cover your topics

Pick blogs that have natural traffic, the traffic you might want to harness using guest posting, which we will get into a little later. It's no use to comment on sites that have little traffic or sites that don't have an interactive online community.

Also, don't be the agent who only comments when he wants to leave a link to his site or content. If you find a site where you want to leave a backlink, endeavor to be a part of that site by commenting on other articles, perhaps shadowing the author (following various social media accounts and even sharing or liking a few of their articles) to increase visibility and build rapport. Shadowing an author will help build up credibility when you eventually reach out to ask for:

1. Them to share your content on Twitter, Facebook, or on their personal blog

2. A guest posting opportunity on their website

3. Their help in a possible collaborative project

Just remember: Use this technique to build occasional backlinks when the content further illustrates the author's point (or rationally disagrees with it), in addition to building relationships that you might want to capitalize on later with other opportunities.

FURTHER READING: BLOG COMMENTING

https://www.quicksprout.com/2012/02/21/an-advanced-guide-to-an-effective-seo-commenting-strategy/

https://smartblogger.com/blog-comments/

http://www.dailyblogtips.com/16-effective-blog-commenting-best-practices/

http://www.fatrank.com/seo-2016-blog-commenting-advanced-guide/

4. FORUMS

Using forums to create backlinks is similar to blog commenting; it's been spammed to death in the past, and the strategy now is more about appearing an expert and generating traffic for your site than being used to rank higher in the search results. An agent can use forums to get backlinks one of three ways:

1. In a profile on the site
2. Within the "signature" of a forum post that may be customizable
3. Within a post to further illustrate or disagree with what's already being discussed

Forums are a way for people to communicate with each other to find solutions to their problems. Of course, the most popular forum for insurance agents is www.insurance-forums.net,[47] but you should also look at other senior forums centered around subjects a senior would want to know more about. Here is a list of some popular forums where agents can help with insurance questions and concerns:

[47] http://www.insurance-forums.net/

http://www.early-retirement.org/forums/

http://www.seniorforums.com/

https://community.aarp.org/

http://www.money-talk.org/board.html

http://www.buzz50.com/

http://mymedicareforum.com/

https://www.agingcare.com/Medicare-Medicaid/Discussions-1

http://www.topix.com

http://www.city-data.com

http://able2know.org/forums/

http://www.ampminsure.org/community/

Agents can also find local forums and message boards to provide answers to people's questions and concerns, while branding themselves as local experts and authorities in the industry. In addition to local forums, check out Quora, Yahoo Answers, and other question-and-answer boards. Sure, it could be time better spent setting appointments or presenting, but if you want to build a strong online brand, you'll find time to contribute or outsource it to an SEO company that specializes in financial and insurance subjects.

FURTHER READING: FORUMS

https://searchenginewatch.com/sew/how-to/2352408/the-10-best-ways-to-generate-traffic-without-google

https://moz.com/blog/qampa-about-using-qampa-sites-to-build-your-business-amp-reputation

https://www.quicksprout.com/2016/03/16/how-to-leverage-qa-sites-to-generate-traffic/

http://blog.wishpond.com/post/65245501112/blog-traffic-how-to-use-q-a-sites-and-niche

5. Copy the Competition

What better way to figure out how to rank for various keywords, than to see what kind of backlinks the competition has already created or earned on their sites for the same keywords? By now, you should have some ideas on what keywords you should be targeting, both generally and locally. Plug your keywords into a search engine (or two) and look for your competitors' websites in the results. Then, you can plug those URLs into a tool that will perform a detailed competitive SEO analysis for you, revealing your competition's business citations, top performing content, media mentions, and other backlinks.

The best three tools to use to dissect competitors' websites are Ahref, Majestic, and SEMRush. Each of these can potentially cost more than hundreds of dollars per month. Many agents' online marketing budgets might be better invested in finding a qualified SEO company (see above) that already has these software tools and the experience to use them. The learning curve gets quite expensive if agents are devoting several months to learn the full capabilities of each tool.

Of course, if the keyword has low traffic or competition (particularly for local searches), then you might not see many or any competitors. This is a huge opportunity for you to craft some content that targets these low competition keywords like we discussed previously, to increase the overall authority of your website, which allows you to compete for more competitive keywords.

Which Links Are Best?

Any one of these tools will serve agents well, but it is up to you to be able to interpret the quality of each link, citation, and mention of the competitors to figure out if the link is:

A. Replicable

B. Placed on a relevant site that has targeted traffic i.e. seniors or baby boomers

C. High or low quality in terms of search engine optimization

Some links may be hard to replicate, like news; while other links are easy to replicate, like business directories, forums, or blog comments. For a more in-depth look at all the reasons why this method isn't foolproof by itself, read Al Gomez's article[48] on the SEMRush blog as he covers the top five reasons why an agent might not be able to (or want to) copy a competitor's back linking strategy.

Another item to note, from Nathan Gotch of www.gotchseo.com,[49] is the ratio of the type of links the current competition is using to rank for these keywords. If the top search result has a ton of guest posts, is listed and linked on multiple sites' resources page, or has multiple mentions from the media regarding life insurance (Final Expense) or Medicare, (and it isn't a government site, Wikipedia, or some other neutral site), it will be tougher to compete with and overtake the number one spot than a competitor whose site mostly has citations and some social media shares.

---

[48] https://www.semrush.com/blog/5-reasons-why-you-cant-always-steal-competitor-backlinks/

[49] http://www.gotchseo.com/

FURTHER READING: COMPETITIVE LINK ANALYSIS

https://ahrefs.com/blog/how-to-get-backlinks/

http://www.robbierichards.com/seo/steal-competitors-backlinks-rankings/

http://neilpatel.com/2015/09/01/the-simple-but-effective-guide-to-keyword-competition-analysis/

6. GUEST POSTING

Guest posting used as a back linking method can help agents be perceived as an expert and earn a high-quality backlink in the process. Throughout the years, this method has been spammed to death, in addition to some of the above linking methods; that's why Google's Matt Cutts warns site owners who pursue this method without considering the quality of the post, the quality of the site, or how the back links are earned.

If agents are going to pursue a guest post opportunity, they should:

A. Research some potential blogs to pitch within their niche.

B. Shadow the potential authors or site owners on their social media channels and blogs — participating, sharing, and complimenting in order to get on their radar.

C. Create the content piece you want to pitch beforehand, tailored to the audience of the site you are pitching.

D. Add in other media elements like quality pictures, a slideshow, a YouTube video, or infographic to lend meaning, explain ideas, and entertain.

Next, agents should reach out to these blog owners and see if they are interested in having you guest blog on their site. Rather than listing guest blog pitching ideas here, visit NinjaOutreach's ultimate guide to blogger outreach with 34 script examples.[50]

The most important point is that the agent will have to create some unique, valuable content that speaks to a blog owner's audience to be considered for this option. Much like prospecting for insurance by buying leads along the cold to warm spectrum, you need to cultivate relationships with potential blogging prospects before presenting your idea to them.

To find these prospects, agents should search for their keyword with additional modifiers like:

- "write for us"
- "guest author/article/post/blogger/contributor"
- "apply to be a contributor"
- "submit an article/article submission"

---

[50] https://ninjaoutreach.com/the-ultimate-guide-to-outreach-scripts/

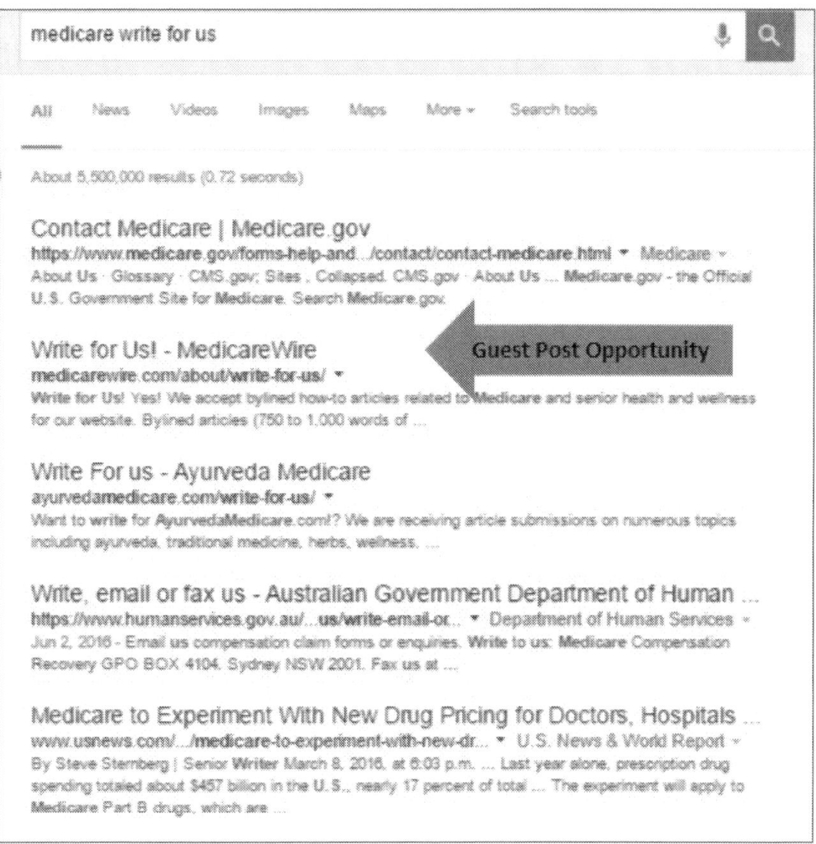

Agents wishing to expand their guest blogging to industry magazines like the ones mentioned above should first create a website with some content, in addition to polishing your social media presence to make the submission process easier. Remember, site owners want to know you can craft engaging and interesting content that also gives readers something they haven't seen anywhere before.

FURTHER READING: GUEST POSTING

https://blog.kissmetrics.com/guide-to-guest-blogging/

http://backlinko.com/the-definitive-guide-to-guest-blogging

https://ahrefs.com/blog/guest-blogging/

7. Resource Links

Building resource links is an advanced but very powerful type of back linking strategy that earns backlinks by being mentioned on another website's content. Whether the content is:

1. Blogged about in "round-ups," "top 10 lists," or "best of" posts
2. Listed as a resource (comparable to the Further Readings found in this section of the book)
3. Used as a replacement for a site's broken link

Being listed as a resource on another site promotes link diversity and traffic, and adds to the authority of the agent's website by being referenced by other sites.

The agent can find opportunities related to the first two types above by searching for their chosen keyword and the words "best," "top," "favorite," along with "links," "resources," "blogs," "sites," "articles," "plans," etc., i.e. "top insurance blogs." The agent can look for top Medicare Supplement plans, or top Final Expense companies, etc. If the agent is willing to try some variations, he can find a list of sites and blogs to shadow and solicit.

To be listed as a resource on another blog, you need a piece (or a series) of content on your website as mentioned above that provides very valuable info by explaining a topic in a helpful or unique way. Then you contact blog owners to ask them to link to it on their resource page.

To find various resource pages, search for your keyword with a modifier like "resources," "helpful links," "useful links," "recommended resources," etc.

Agents should also try local keywords to find any local lists they might want to be added to. Also, be sure to check out the Further Reading section for more search examples to help agents look for additional resource link opportunities.

The last option to obtain a resource link — by helping a site owner replace a broken link on his website with one of yours — can be very lucrative for an agent, especially if he utilizes Brian Dean's "Moving Man Method."[51] The majority of agents reading this are probably wondering why site owners would want to link to your site rather than ignore the broken link. The reason why site owners should monitor their sites (*ahem*) and repair any broken links is because that is a **ranking factor** for some search engine's algorithms. Search engines look unfavorably on sites that have broken links, so why not help a fellow site owner out while helping out their audience by offering missing information?

The agent can go about this one of two ways (there's actually three), explained by Neil Patel in his article "A Step by Step Guide to Modern Broken Link Building."[52] You can start with a list of sites that have enough traffic and cover similar topics or write for the same audience, or you can create stellar content (hopefully centered around some keywords) and then find the sites to pitch to. Either way, you will have to use a free tool like Screaming Frog or other free web browser extensions that enable you to analyze a site for broken links, which are no longer responsive (could be because they changed domains, discontinued the site, etc.). Lastly, agents wishing to utilize broken link building should capitalize their time and effort by looking for other sites that have linked to the same

---

51 http://backlinko.com/high-quality-backlinks

52 https://www.quicksprout.com/2015/08/19/a-step-by-step-guide-to-modern-broken-link-building/

(broken) page. Chances are if one site links to a site or page as a resource, then other sites see the authoritative mention and likewise link to it. If you find a broken resource link, you can probably find other sites that have also linked to it, and help them all out by offering your content as a replacement resource link. This turns one opportunity into multiple resource links, which is called the "Moving Man Method" by Backlinko's Brian Dean.

Hopefully we didn't lose you on this link building tactic. It's rather advanced, and it's useful for getting links within a person's resource page or replacing one of their broken links that talks about insurance. Of course using archive.org to see what the page was about, updating the info, and expanding upon the information in a long authoritative post is surely going to earn some links from a site or two.

If you can find a site that has been linked to quite a few times, this technique can yield a low cost per backlink earned, while expanding your site's reputation as a resource. Again, this is a very advanced technique, and is better left to an SEO agency working on your behalf. At least now you can talk to them on the subject instead of wandering in the dark when they bring up "broken link building" as a way to get your site ranking in the search engines.

FURTHER READING: RESOURCE LINKS

http://backlinko.com/high-quality-backlinks

http://citationlabs.com/36-broken-link-building-resources/

http://www.buzzstream.com/blog/resource-page-links.html

8. PR AND HARO

One tried-and-true way to exhibit your knowledge and be seen as an expert in your industry is by getting favorable mentions in the media. Media mentions and links can be very powerful, not only for local rankings within the "3-pack" but also for organic keyword rankings as well. This is especially true now that the Google Panda algorithm has altered the search engine results so that professionals/companies/brands with more media mentions rank higher, as explained by Simon Penson in a previous article on Moz.[53] What better way to inspire trust and be displayed as an expert than to be mentioned by local, national, or industry journalists and bloggers?

Agents can go about getting media mentions two ways: you can create a piece of groundbreaking or valuable content covering a timely topic that you think various media would like to cover, or you can seek out journalists or bloggers and be a readily available resource for them if they need an insurance expert later for a certain article idea they have. Either way, agents need to craft a plan if they're seeking to be included by the media as a source.

If you're going the first route, you will have to:

1. Come up with content ideas by thinking like an editor: focusing on industry trends, timely news, and human interest stories.

2. Create the content.

3. Find journalists or influencers within your industry (Medicare, insurance, finance, senior lifestyle, retirement, etc.)

4. Pitch the journalists to see if they might be interested in covering the topic you wrote about, offering a link to your content.

5. Follow up until you get some "media traction."

---

[53] https://moz.com/blog/panda-patent-brand-mentions

It almost sounds like ... selling insurance via interruptive marketing techniques!

The second route the agent can take is to make himself available to journalists or influencers that often cover related topics. The best tool an agent can use to make himself available as a professional source is HARO (Help A Reporter Out). This free platform matches up reporters seeking resources for their upcoming articles with experts in a given field. If the agent is quick enough to respond (remember, these reporters are on deadline!) and can display expertise in the industry, his chances of being used as a source for an article or news story increase.

The majority of agents don't have time to constantly peruse and pursue potential media opportunities, between creating the content to display expertise by providing value that's newsworthy, and contacting and following up with industry bloggers or journalists. A good way to establish credibility, get yourself in news or trade publications, and obtain these possible backlinks is to outsource this to a PR firm[54] or consultant that is well-versed with content creation and SEO.

Agents can't just outsource this avenue of link building to an average SEO company; they need to find one that is versed in PR/media relations and financial (technical) content creation as well, to complete the loop. The majority of SEO companies can pitch industry insiders and build links all day long, but unless they have an award-winning reputation paired with the content creation skills necessary to attain these brand-defining mentions, then they'll only take you halfway to your goal. You may want to wait until you find a more experienced company, than to have an agency learn on your dollar when it comes to this authority building technique.

---

[54] http://www.bantamedia.com/

If you're a DIY-type of agent, the best tools we recommend for finding these media prospects include Citation Lab's Link Prospector[55] that can compile this information for a price. We also recommend using BuzzSumo and Ninja Outreach to find the contact info for these prospects, in addition to following up with them.

After embarking on a PR campaign, being featured in an article, or sending out a press release, you may find mentions of yourself or your agency, but without a backlink. A lot of good that does. You can email the site owner or the author and ask politely to add a reference link to the story or article. Some sites or authors may oblige; some may not want to link directly to your website but may opt for a social media profile from a site like LinkedIn. For more on unlinked brand mentions, look at the Ahref's article in the Further Reading section below.

FURTHER READING: PR & HARO

https://moz.com/blog/92-ways-to-get-and-maximize-press-coverage

http://citationlabs.com/local-marketing-engagement-guide/

https://ahrefs.com/blog/haro-link-building/

https://www.quicksprout.com/university/how-to-get-exposure-and-links-using-haro/

http://www.bthinkforward.com/haro/

http://heroicsearch.com/how-to-use-haro-for-links-mentions/

https://ahrefs.com/blog/simple-guide-turning-unlinked-brand-mentions-links/

---

[55] http://citationlabs.com/tools/link-prospector/

http://searchengineland.com/press-requests-can-link-building-gold-mine-195909

Protect Your Online Brand Reputation

Before we end the online branding section, we would like to impart a word of warning to agents who opt for cheaper and quicker ways of ranking their websites and building their online brands. Cultivating a brand and a positive online reputation takes years, and can take only days to ruin. Search engine algorithms update all the time; what may work today may not work — and may even be considered spammy — tomorrow.

That's why we recommend being very careful before hiring SEO companies to do any work on behalf of your brand reputation. This can be especially true if they are:

A. Promising you first page results (which can never can be guaranteed)

B. Suspiciously cheap

C. Inexperienced at reaching out to large brands/companies, influencers, or media figures to cultivate the most valuable links needed in a competitive industry like insurance.

The Use of PBN's and Other Quick Rank Schemes

A Private Blog Network (PBN) is a network of domains arranged on different servers to look independent, although they're all used covertly to build links to a main money-making site, with the goal of boosting its search engine rankings. This sneaky strategy gives sites a head-start to ranking by using expired domains that have built up some trust, if only because of their age. Unfortunately, these types of sites don't usually feature quality content to attract engaged audiences, or much traffic at all. Plus, resurrecting an old site just for a backlink violates Google's rules, so it will penalize any sites discovered to be part of these networks.

Our advice? It's not worth it. Do not be tempted to use these. The price may be amazing, and the rankings may work – for a while. Unfortunately, there have been many experienced SEO experts who have been lured by cheap and quick results with PBN's, who've had their entire sites deindexed and then had to start from scratch.

Here's a list of other techniques to watch out for:

- Press Releases to low-quality or free sites
- Guest Posts to PBN's
- Using hundreds of random 2.0 sites
- Using low-quality videos to rank on Youtube
- Buying thousands of links on Fiverr or other forums

This is just a sample of shady offerings we see that tempt the impatient. Remember this is a long-term strategy, ranking in the search engine for keywords, and it shouldn't be rushed with poor quality content **OR** links.

Online Branding Section Conclusion

Now that we have our final warning out of the way, we want to reiterate that building an online brand enables an agent to earn more clients by:

1. Inspiring trust in prospects researching him (especially when he first calls or leaves a message).
2. Looking referable to his current clients who may be hesitant about providing referrals.
3. Being found by seniors online searching for keywords or phrases that the agent targets with his site or content.

If the agent wants to increase and obtain all three, then he must set up a website with unique and valuable content that is promoted with a variety of link building methods. After a consistent effort (either by the agent or the SEO company working on behalf of the agent), you can start to rank for low competition terms while aiming for more competitive terms. After a year or so (and after reading some of the sources above), the agent will start to receive leads, increased callbacks, and more referrals, thanks to their internet search engine rankings.

FURTHER READING: OTHER LINK-BUILDING RESOURCES

https://ahrefs.com/blog/how-to-get-backlinks/

http://www.whitespark.ca/blog/post/77-how-to-find-opportunities-for-local-link-building

https://blog.hubspot.com/blog/tabid/6307/bid/32479/32-White-Hat-Ways-to-Build-Inbound-Links.aspx

https://ahrefs.com/blog/local-seo/

http://audiencestack.com/static/blog-the-ultimate-list-of-50-link-building-strategies.html

http://pointblankseo.com/link-building-strategies

https://ahrefs.com/blog/seo-techniques/

http://startbloggingonline.com/how-to-promote-your-blog-and-get-visitors/

https://ahrefs.com/blog/white-hat-link-building-expert-roundup/#Nate_Shivar

https://www.distilled.net/linkbait-guide/

CONCLUSION

The agent reading this book is now armed with:

- ✓ The differences between selling Final Expense life insurance and Medicare Supplements
- ✓ The seven types of lead options when it comes to prospecting for clients
- ✓ What to say to leads that will enable him to present their options, whether for Final Expense or Medigap plans
- ✓ How to address objections and overcome hesitation from leads
- ✓ What to do to keep his clients happy after he sells them a policy
- ✓ How to cross-sell clients on other types of insurance and earn referrals
- ✓ Ways to build and showcase an online brand

If an agent cannot convert a particular lead, he now knows how to turn leads that aren't ready yet into pipeline leads, so he can follow up with them at a later time (perhaps after a rate increase or after someone close to them passes away). Cross-selling and following up on pipeline leads, in addition to acquiring fresh leads, will help an agent sell more and spend less on leads.

We would also like to take a moment to thank all of the contributors who took the time to help out other agents in the insurance industry by answering our calls for collaboration on this book.

COLLABORATORS

1. Glen Shelton	http://www.leadheroes.com/
2. Justin Bilyj	http://www.ohiomedicareplans.com/
3. Todd Graves	http://burialinsurancenow.com/
4. Matt Mungia, MBA	http://theinsurancesquad.com
5. Mike Smith	http://garrickinsurance.com/
6. Jason Eichmiller	http://www.integratedfin.com/
7. Todd R. King	https://www.trkingim.com/
8. Debbie Majher	http://majherinsurance.com/
9. Loran Marmes	http://medicaresolutionsteam.com/
10. Garrett Ball	http://medicare-supplement-comparison.com/
11. Jason McKenzie	http://medicaresupplementshops.com/
12. Tom Massey	http://medicaresupplementsandmore.com/
13. Carlos Guillen	http://socalburialinsurance.com/
14. Bob Vineyard	http://www.georgia-medicareplans.com/
15. Jeff Cornelius	
16. Ron Wiza	
17. Robin Penrod	
18. Mark Barendt	
19. Frank Bahr	
20. William Hankins	
21. Brandon Webster	
22. Nathan Robinson	
23. Ed Murphy	
24. Lawrence Malone	
25. Jeff Erb	

26. Philip Arko	
27. Tamara Sasso	
28. Mary Dioguardi	
29. Mike Shure	
30. Denise Rangel	
31. Joseph Smith	
32. Josh Doe	
33. Joe Erazo	
34. Chris Fonner	
35. Ron Van Deusen	

We hope you enjoyed reading this guide. Please be sure to check out our website where we will go more in-depth with some of the resources we briefly covered within this guide as the year goes on.

If you're ready to put the strategies and scripts from this book into practice by helping seniors find more affordable life insurance and Medicare solutions, we'd like to help. Lead Heroes is extending a 15% discount to first-time customers who order telemarketed insurance leads from us using the promo code "**BOOK15.**" Visit our website, http://www.leadheroes.com, for more information on our lead generation programs, in addition to more resources similar to this guide.

Made in the USA
Columbia, SC
05 April 2022

58557207R00139